Recipes From
The English Market

First published in 2012 by Atrium
Atrium is an imprint of Cork University Press
Youngline Industrial Estate, Pouladuff Road, Togher, Cork, Ireland

Text © Michelle Horgan
Images © the photographers as per page number below –
Louis Eden: 9, 70, 136, 197, 207.
Jedrzej Niezgoda: xvi, xix, xx, 1, 9 (top), 17, 19, 33, 39, 59 (bottom), 65 (bottom), 73, 79, 83, 93 (bottom), 102, 103, 105, 109, 112, 113, 115 (bottom), 121, 125 (left), 133 (top, left), 139, 148-151 (background), 149, 153 (bottom), 157 (top), 167, 173, 179, 183 (top), 189, 197 (top), 198, 199, 201, 209, 213, 217, 228, 231, 239, 243, 249, 250, 251, 253, 256, 261, 271 (top), 274, 278-279 (background), 279, 281, 283, 294
Jason Town: iv, viii, xiv, 2, 4, 7, 15, 20, 23, 27, 35, 36, 41, 45, 46, 49, 50, 53, 54, 57, 59, 61, 62, 65, 67, 73, 75, 76, 81, 86, 91, 93, 94, 95, 97, 98, 101, 106, 111, 115, 123, 125, 126, 129, 131, 133, 135, 141, 144, 147, 151, 154, 155, 157, 159, 160, 163, 169, 170, 174, 177, 181, 183, 185, 186, 194, 214, 218, 221, 223, 224, 225, 227, 233, 241, 246, 255, 259, 267, 268, 281, 284, 287, 293.
Bord Bia: 11, 87, 151, 204, 214.

British Library Cataloguing in Publication Data

A CIP catalogue record for this book is available from the British Library.

ISBN 978-1855942-22-6

Book design and typesetting, Anú Design, Tara
Printed in Malta by Gutenberg Press

For all Atrium books visit www.corkuniversitypress.com

Recipes From The English Market

EDITED AND WRITTEN BY

MICHELLE HORGAN

ATRIUM

For Jennifer, Hazel, Grace and Jeanann,

with love always xxxx

English Market Menu*

A plate of English Market tapas consisting of:
Marinated olives
Selection of warm breads with dipping oils
Trio of heavenly Munster cheeses
Sweet and salted almonds
White pudding and orchard apple tartlet
Crispy pork belly scratchings

Roast garlic quails wrapped in bacon and served with baby potatoes and watercress salad
Tripe and drisheen tartlets with caramelised red onion
Skirts and kidney pie
Seared Ballycotton scallops with rashers of bacon in an Irish whiskey cream sauce
Crúbeen, parsley and thyme potato cakes
Paddy's Irish onion soup with fried bread
Bone marrow with boxty
Bacon and cabbage soup with mustard
Salad of spiced beef with roasted pears and Cooleeny cheese
William's seafood chowder

Irish lamb stew served with a thyme and red onion scone
Ashley O'Neill's rib-eye steak with red wine reduction, balsamic onions and hand-cut potato chips
Red mullet with sautéed pak choi
Michael Bresnan's beef casserole with Murphy's Stout

Wild rabbit stew with pasta and Parmesan shavings
O'Connell's lemon sole fillets stuffed with Dublin Bay prawns
Roast goose with Bramley apples and prunes
Roast haddock with champ
Stephen Landon's smoked bacon with savoy cabbage and buttered carrots
Butterflied forequarter of lamb with rosemary and thyme
Pan-fried hake with lemon and herb-butter sauce
Apricot-stuffed belly of pork
Royal korma Mr Bell style
Coughlan's corned mutton with a caper sauce

Hadji Bey's turkish delight ice-cream terrine
Mr Bell's orange blossom and cardamom cake
Bubble Brothers' champagne jelly
Irish coffee cupcakes
Rose Daly's pear and chocolate tart
Carrageen pudding with honey and nutmeg
Baked figs with sticky orange glaze
Strawberries dipped in chocolate
Lavender custard with honey and berries

Selection of Cork cheeses
Irish coffee

* All ingredients from the English Market Menu may be purchased within the market.

Contents

Introduction

The English Market is a Cork institution and one of my favourite places in Ireland to shop. As soon as you walk in you can feel the energy of the place, the hustle and bustle as traders and customers exchange not just food but advice and stories. I am always inspired by what's on offer there, immediately wanting to gather up ingredients to cook with or eat some of the delicious food being prepared.

The English Market has such an exciting melting-pot of different cultures all under one roof. There are the second- and third-generation butchers selling tripe and drisheen, as well as the more exotic stalls selling ingredients from Asia or further afield. At its core, the difference between a market stall and shop comes down to the interaction between seller and customer. Each seller is an expert in what they're making and selling, and the advice they offer is the product of years of experience. With all those stalls in the market, this makes for a real wealth of experience! Thankfully, this book has finally distilled all that expertise and knowledge to bring you a collection of wonderful recipes from so many of the well-loved traders. This recipe collection is as eclectic as the market itself, with food ranging from the traditional to the obscure. It is a piece of Cork history and a book to treasure.

Rachel

Rachel Allen

The Origins of the English Market

Cork's English Market, Ireland's most famous food emporium, dates back to 1788. It is a 'covered' or indoor market which occupies a large site between the Grand Parade, Patrick Street, Marlborough Street and Oliver Plunkett Street. As it can be accessed from all of these streets, the English Market could aptly be described as an enormous 'chest cavity' which houses the very heart of Cork city.

For the visitor, there is no better way to get an instant 'snapshot' of Cork than to proceed immediately to the English Market. It is the perfect way to discover what the essence of the city and its people are all about. Banter, good humour and even the odd jibe, delivered with the intention of bringing the recipient back down to earth if they are exhibiting signs of loftiness, are all elements of the Cork persona. If Cork city were a person, he or she would be formed using little elements of each of the stallholders in the English Market.

So why 'the *English* Market'?

The first question almost everybody asks is – how did the Market get its name? Why is this wonderful showcase *Irish* market called the *English* Market? To understand this dichotomy we have to go back in time and delve a little into the history books.

Back in the eighteenth century, Ireland was populated quite densely with English settlers. The poorer 'natives' were kept out of the cities, and trade and prosperity were enjoyed only by the wealthier classes – in this case, the English and their descendants. At this time in Ireland, and even as far back as the mid-1600s, a large number of native Irish landowners had been evicted from their own farms and their properties were taken over by English settlers. Not only was most of the land and property in the hands of the English, even though they were in the minority (Catholics made up over eighty per cent of the population), but all positions of authority also lay with the English Protestants. The native Irish Catholics did not have a vote and they could not become members of the city's corporation or of parliament.

In the last half of the eighteenth century, when the English Market first opened its doors, most food provisions were bought at markets in the centre of towns, and in this regard, Cork was no different. In Cork city centre in the late 1700s there was a fish market, a herb market, several meat markets, a corn market, several milk and butter markets as well as potato markets, vegetable markets, fruit markets and, of course, Cork's very famous and world-renowned Butter Exchange. As there was no refrigeration at this time, provisions had to be bought on a daily basis. Mid-morning was a particularly busy time in the city as shoppers, housemaids and cooks all jostled to make their daily purchases.

These markets, or 'shambles' as they were called, were indeed just that – a total shambles! They did not remotely resemble the attractive market stalls that we are accustomed to today, but were higgledy-piggledy gatherings of traders vying to sell their wares on the side of the streets. They were dirty and unhygienic and, not infrequently, at the meat shambles, animals were slaughtered at the side of the street, allowing blood and intestines to spill out on to the cobbles!

But this unflattering portrait of life in the eighteenth century was not exclusive to Cork. An account given by an Italian visitor to London in the 1700s states: *'The streets are badly paved, filled with mud black as ink and with every kind of filth. It is difficult, unless you are very active upon your feet, to get out of the way of all the horses and carriages which, even if they do not actually touch you, cover your coat with ugly splashes.'* And a Pastor Moritz gives another testimony which resembles similar accounts given of Cork at this time: *'Nothing in London makes so disgusting an appearance to a foreigner as the butcher's shops, especially in the environs of the town. Guts and all the nastiness are thrown into the middle of the street and cause an intolerable stench.'**

And so, in an effort to clean up the city of Cork, the corporation made compulsory purchase orders on a number of buildings on the Grand Parade. The city fathers envisaged an attractive indoor market with uniform stalls, which would be pleasing to the eye. This new indoor market would go a long way towards taking the sale of perishable produce off the streets so that they could be sold in a more hygienic and controlled way.

The new flagship market officially opened its doors for business in July 1788 and it was initially known as the New Market; then later on it was referred to as the Corporation Market, and yet another name change came later on when it was called the Grand Parade Market. Several stalls were offered for rent by the corporation and it was stipulated that the stalls were to be used for the sale of meat only. It would take several more years for the market to be completed in full, and by that time the market extended from the Grand Parade to Princes Street, and included fish stalls, vegetable and fowl stalls. It is likely that the name 'English Market' came about as the poorer Catholic Irish used the term to differentiate between this more affluent market and the other poorer markets in the city which were frequented by them.

To place the year 1788 in a worldwide context, that was the year that:
- On 18 January: the first ship arrived in Botany Bay to colonise Australia.
- On 7 June in France: The Day of Tiles – considered to be the beginning of the French Revolution.
- On 1 August: the official opening of the English Market in Cork.
- On 10 August in Vienna: Wolfgang Amadeus Mozart completed his final symphony.

* *Taken from* 'Travellers in Eighteenth-Century England', *by Rosamond Bayne-Powell.*

English Market stallholders and staff.

Essential Cook's Information

TEMPERATURE

Degrees Celsius	Gas Mark
110	¼
130	½
140	1
150	2
170	3
180	4
190	5
200	6
220	7
230	8
240	9

MEASURES

Metric	Imperial
5mm	¼ inch
1cm	½ inch
2cm	¾ inch
2.5cm	1 inch
3cm	1¼ inches
4cm	1½ inches
5cm	2 inches
7.5cm	3 inches
10cm	4 inches
15cm	6 inches
18cm	7 inches
20.5cm	8 inches
23cm	9 inches
25.5cm	10 inches
28cm	11 inches
30.5cm	12 inches

WEIGHTS

Metric	Imperial
15g	½oz
25g	1oz
40g	1½oz
50g	2oz
75g	3oz
100g	3½oz
125g	4oz
150g	5oz
175g	6oz
200g	7oz
225g	8oz
250g	9oz
275g	10oz
300g	11oz
350g	12oz
375g	13oz
400g	14oz
425g	15oz
450g	1lb
550g	1¼lb
700g	1½lb
900g	2lb
1.1kg	2½lb

LIQUIDS

Metric	Imperial
5ml	1 tsp
15ml	1 tbsp
25ml	1fl oz
50ml	2fl oz
100ml	3½fl oz
125ml	4fl oz
150ml	5fl oz (¼ pint)
175ml	6fl oz
200ml	7fl oz
250ml	9fl oz
300ml	½ pint
500ml	18fl oz
600ml	1 pint
900ml	1½ pints
1 litre	1¾ pints

Remember, fan ovens are slightly hotter than other types of ovens – you may need to adjust/lower the temperature accordingly and always preheat your oven/grill to the specified temperature before cooking.

Use one set of measurements – never mix metric and imperial.

All spoon measures are level, unless otherwise stated.

All eggs are large, unless otherwise stated.

A. O'Reilly and Sons

Stall 1

Donagh O'Reilly is the third generation of tripe producers in his family and one of only a few left in Ireland. It is O'Reilly's tripe that supplies outlets in Cork, Limerick and Dublin. The O'Reilly family also makes and supplies black pudding and white pudding. Recently, they reintroduced an old family recipe, a black pudding made from fresh produce with a delicious blend of added cereals. They also make white pudding using organic barley, and both puddings are available to buy from the O'Reilly stall in the English Market. Also featured at the English Market stall are a variety of artisan sausages produced from old family recipes, some now incorporating newer continental flavours. Pies are handmade on site each morning using O'Reillys' best pork.

Tripe is part of the robust traditional cooking of many countries throughout the world. In Taiwan it is cooked with black beans and ginger, while in Istanbul tripe soup is a popular dish.

In Ireland tripe recipes are credited with having great restorative powers after a night out! Among many old English recipe books you can find various tripe recipes listed, from *Tripe à l'Anglaise*, dipped in breadcrumbs and fried, to classical Roman recipes, and tripe with honey and ginger.

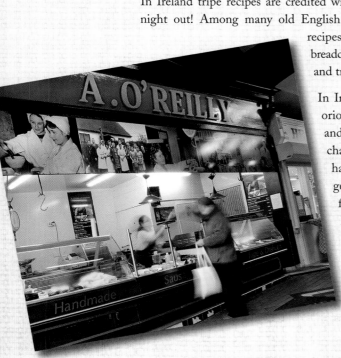

In Ireland, tripe is usually sold dressed, a laborious process which requires much stripping and cleaning before hours of boiling in several changes of water. In Cork, the O'Reilly family have perfected this preparation over many generations and have traded dressed tripe for over 100 years from their stall at the English Market.

1

Tartlets of O'Reilly's Tripe and Drisheen with Caramelised Red Onion

A favourite of many Irish people, this is a traditional tripe and drisheen recipe with a modern twist. Great to serve as a 'nibble' with drinks, or as an innovative starter.

Makes 12 tartlets

For the tartlets
275g/10oz plain flour
150g/5oz margarine or butter
pinch of salt
cold water to bind the flour and butter mixture into a dough

Place the flour in a large bowl and add the margarine, cut into cubes. Rub the margarine into the flour until it resembles fine breadcrumbs. Slowly add the cold water, a little at a time, stirring the mixture as you do so. When you have added enough water the flour mixture will form a ball of dough. Knead the dough on a floured board or table and roll it out until it is thin enough to line the bottom of a queen cake tin or tartlet cases which have already been buttered. Cut each tartlet out of the rolled-out pastry with a 5cm/2in in pastry cutter or a glass turned upside down and place each tartlet into the bun mould. Cover each tartlet with a little greaseproof paper and fill with baking beans or a little uncooked rice. This will ensure that the pastry is covered and weighed down so that it cannot brown or bubble up. This process is known as 'baking blind'. Cook for approximately 10–12 minutes in the centre of the oven until just cooked. Take out and leave to cool.

For the tripe and sauce filling
300g/11oz tripe, cut into bite-sized pieces
salt and ground black pepper
200g/7oz crème fraîche
1 red onion, peeled and sliced
small bunch of parsley, finely chopped
½ tsp celery seed

Bring a pot of water to the boil, add the tripe and allow to simmer for 20 minutes. Drain the water and then add the crème fraîche and half of the sliced onion. Fry the other sliced onion in a little oil until it is caramelised and put it aside to be used as a garnish later on. Allow the chopped onion and crème fraîche to simmer for a few minutes.

Add salt and ground black pepper and some celery seed if you wish for extra flavour. If you feel that the sauce is a little too thick, add a little milk to make it more liquid. Finally, add a little drisheen chopped into bitesized pieces to the sauce and leave to simmer for a couple of minutes until thoroughly heated.

Drisheen

In Cork it is traditional to add some drisheen to the tripe dish before serving. Drisheen (a fresh blood pudding) is a Cork food speciality that is produced by the O' Reilly family and is unique in feature and characteristic depending on the products, geographical origin and source. The drisheen only requires heating and may be added to the tripe for simmering two minutes before serving. Drisheen may also be served fried or boiled in milk and seasoned with salt and pepper. Add fresh chopped herbs to the drisheen for an extra lift.

To assemble the tartlets

Put a spoonful of the tripe and drisheen mixture into each pastry case. Top with caramelised red onion and a sprinkle of chopped parsley.

Tripe with Honey and Ginger Sauce

A new way to enjoy tripe – something totally out of the ordinary.

Serves 4

680g/1½ lb tripe
25g/1 oz butter
¼ tsp ground black pepper
½ tsp freshly grated ginger
1 tsp celery seed
1 tsp honey
2 tsp sherry vinegar
280ml/½ pint beef stock (a cube will do if you haven't time to make beef stock)
handful of parsley, chopped

Rinse and dry the tripe thoroughly and cut it into 5cm/2-inch squares. Melt the butter in a large frying pan, fry the tripe in it and sprinkle on the pepper, ginger and celery seed.

Cook for 5 minutes then add the honey, vinegar and stock. Bring to the boil, skim the surface and simmer for 20 minutes.

Add the parsley, season to taste and cook for 15–20 minutes more.

Serve with rice.

White Pudding and Orchard Apple Tartlets

These delicious tartlets are great served as part of an English Market 'tapas' plate. Serve along with your favourite cheeses, olives and breads for a very delicious and totally different starter before a special meal.

For the tartlets
275g/10oz plain flour
150g/5oz margarine or butter
pinch of salt
cold water to bind the flour and butter mixture into a dough

Place the flour in a large bowl and add the margarine, cut into cubes. Rub the margarine into the flour until it resembles fine breadcrumbs. Slowly add the cold water, a little at a time, stirring the mixture as you do so. When you have added enough water, the flour mixture will form a ball of dough. Knead the dough on a floured board or table and roll it out until it is thin enough to line the bottom of a queen cake or bun baking tray which has already been buttered. Cut each tartlet out of the rolled-out pastry with a 5cm/2in pastry cutter or a glass turned upside down and place the pastry into the bun or tartlet case. Cover each tartlet with a little baking parchment paper and fill with baking beans or a little uncooked rice. This will ensure that the pastry is covered and weighed down so that it cannot brown nor bubble up. This process is known as 'baking blind'. Cook for approximately 10–12 minutes in the centre of the oven until just cooked. Take out and leave to cool.

For the filling
1 O'Reilly white pudding
2 medium cooking apples
1½ tbsp sugar

Peel and slice the apples and cook them over a low/medium heat in a covered saucepan with 1 tablespoon of water. When softened, add the sugar and stir.

Slice the white pudding into 3cm-thick slices. Grill the white pudding slices for about 2 minutes per side.

Assembly
Put a tablespoon of apple in each tartlet case and top with 2 slices of the white pudding. Put the tartlets back in the oven for about 5 minutes, or microwave for about 2 minutes to warm slightly before serving.

Café Anraith

Stall 4B

*A*nraith is the Irish word for soup, and this is appropriate, as Café Anraith is best known for its delicious spicy lentil soup. Cork office workers form orderly lines for owner Caroline Murphy's delicious soup and brown bread. 'We may be small but this just means that we can focus on every customer and get to know them on the way,' says Caroline.

Both of Caroline's parents came from Irish-speaking areas, and this instilled in her a love of her native language from a young age. In 2010 she received the Pádraig Ó Cuanacháin Irish Language in Business Award. Caroline is open for business at 8am each morning and serves hearty Irish breakfasts to Corkonians in need of an early-morning boost. Her homemade pancakes are legendary, and her bowls of organic oatmeal with fresh berries, honey and cream will set you up for the day. Caroline's sandwiches, cakes and soups contain no artificial colours or preservatives.

In 2011 French patissière Angélique Malezieux joined Caroline in the café. Angélique, who grew up in the Champagne region of France and studied at the National Institute of Patisserie and Boulangerie in France, bakes delicious fresh cakes, pies and tarts every day and these have proved to be very popular with customers.

Organic Oatmeal with West Cork Honey and Cream

'People can be very particular about how their oatmeal is cooked – it's just one of those things that people tend to have very fixed opinions on,' Caroline says. However, she has received no complaints about the oatmeal she serves in her café, only compliments, so she must be doing something right.

Serves 1

40g/1½oz Flahavans Organic Oatmeal
170ml/6fl oz milk or water
West Cork honey
fresh cream

Stir the oats into the milk or water.

Bring to the boil and cook briskly for 3 minutes, stirring all the time. Cooking time will be reduced if the oats are soaked in just enough cold water to barely cover them overnight.

Caroline serves her oatmeal with a handful of fresh berries (blueberries, raspberries and halved strawberries), a tablespoon of honey drizzled over the top and a tablespoon of fresh cream poured around the side of the bowl. A delicious and healthy way to start the day.

Caroline recommends using a deep bowl and allowing over an inch at the top of the bowl for the oats to expand during the cooking process.

Café Anraith Perfect Pancakes

Delicious, light, wafer-thin pancakes, served with your favourite filling. This recipe makes perfect pancakes every time.

Makes about 8

125g/4oz plain flour
pinch of salt
1 egg plus 1 egg yolk
2 tbsp cold water
225ml/8fl oz whole or semi-skimmed milk
small knob of butter

Sift the flour into a large mixing bowl and add a pinch of salt. Make a well in the centre, and pour the egg and the yolk into it. Mix the milk with 2 tbsp water and then pour a little in with the egg and beat together.

Whisk the flour into the liquid ingredients, drawing it gradually into the middle until you have a smooth paste the consistency of double cream. Whisk in the rest of the milk until the batter is more like single cream. Cover and refrigerate for at least half an hour.

Heat the butter in a frying pan on a medium-high heat. You only need enough fat to grease the bottom of the pan. It should be hot enough that the batter sizzles when it hits it.

Spread a small ladleful of batter across the bottom of the pan, quickly swirling to coat. When it begins to set, loosen the edges with a thin spatula or palette knife. When it begins to colour on the bottom, flip it over with the same instrument and cook for another 30 seconds.

Pancakes are best eaten as soon as possible, otherwise they go rubbery. If you're cooking for a crowd, keep them separate until you're ready to serve them by layering them up between pieces of greaseproof paper.

Caroline suggests serving the pancakes with fresh berries, sliced banana and maple syrup. As an alternative, she offers her pancakes covered with chocolate spread and chopped hazelnuts.

Café Anraith Spicy Lentil Soup

Something a little out of the ordinary. A great fortifying soup for a cold winter's day.

1 large onion, chopped
rapeseed oil for frying
2 cloves of garlic
1 large potato, cubed
200g/7oz of lentils (red split or green puy), washed
1 tsp turmeric
1 tsp cumin
1 tsp dried chilli flakes
1 litre/1¾ pints vegetable stock
1 400g/14oz can of coconut milk or coconut cream
1 fresh chilli
fresh coriander to garnish

Peel and dice the onion and fry in a large saucepan with a little rapeseed oil.

Using a micro-plane, grate the 2 cloves of garlic and add to the onion. (You can also roast the garlic first, if you like, as this gives a lovely sweetness.) When the onions are well cooked, add the turmeric, cumin and chilli flakes and stir in to release the flavours.

Next, add the vegetable stock and finally the cubed potatoes. Stir well. Bring the soup to the boil and then add the washed lentils and simmer for 20 minutes. Add the coconut milk and the fresh chilli. Serve with a generous sprig of coriander.

Kathleen Noonan

Stall 21

Kathleen Noonan never retired, but passed away at the age of 86 in 2007 after a brief illness. She worked at her stall in the English Market up until the very end, because that was the kind of woman she was. Her daughter, Pauline, then stepped in to run the stall on a full-time basis and is now also assisted at weekends by her own daughter, Katie. Katie was the ripe old age of two weeks when she first joined her mother at the stall, spending a few hours every Saturday in her baby rocker behind the counter. Even now, on Mondays and Tuesdays when business is slow, Katie comes to the stall after school and does her homework, which is supervised by her mum, Pauline.

'My mother was a great woman,' says Pauline. 'She would put myself and my brother in our pram when we were small and we would all go and pick up the meat for the stall together. The meat would be parcelled up in brown paper and she would put it in the carrier tray at the bottom of the pram and push us all back into town. My mother used to frequently say that the only part of the pig that she didn't sell was its squeal!'

Pauline now continues the family tradition of supplying the people of Cork with the most traditional of offal dishes, which used to be the mainstay of many households in days gone by. Pauline sells skirts (the pig's oesophagus, which is delicious, tasty and tender after a few hours of slow cooking), kidneys, bodice (bacon ribs which have been 'salted' or corned, like corned beef), spare ribs, pork hock, ham hock, pork steak, sausages, rashers, black and white puddings, bacon and ham fillets. Also very popular are pigs' tails, crúbeen (trotters) and pigs' heads. Lately, Pauline has noticed an increase in demand for these old-fashioned favourites, with one or two of the 'trendier' restaurants in the city offering deep-fried pigs' tails and crúbeen on Cork 'tapas' plates.

Pauline Noonan's Spare Ribs, English Market Style

This is Pauline's favourite TV snack when watching the big games with all the family. Monumentally delicious Cork finger food.

Serves 4

2 spare ribs
6 potatoes, boiled and mashed with salt, pepper, butter and milk
1 large sprig of thyme
a handful of chopped parsley
1 onion, chopped and lightly-fried

Place one of the spare ribs in a foil-lined roasting dish.

To the cooked and mashed potatoes, add the chopped thyme, parsley and lightly fried onion. Place this potato stuffing directly on top of the spare rib and then cover the stuffing with the other spare rib placed on top. Pour Pauline's two-minute marinade (page 25) over the top of the spare ribs. Cover the roasting dish with tin foil and roast in a moderately hot oven (200°C/390°F/gas mark 7) for 30 minutes. Then remove the tin foil from the top of the roasting dish and roast for another 30 minutes.

Spare ribs are also nice marinated overnight and baked in the oven or put straight on to the barbecue.

Kathleen Noonan's Recipe for Crúbeens

This is Pauline's mother's recipe for crúbeens – another original Cork recipe.

Serves 4

4 crúbeens (1 per person)
2 large parsnips

Place the crúbeens in a pot of cold water and bring to the boil. Simmer for 2½ to 3 hours. Remove the crúbeens from the pot and cook the parsnips in the crúbeen water.

The parsnips should be served to the side of the crúbeens.

Pauline Noonan's Skirts and Kidney Pies

Very delicious pies – one is never enough. Ideally, start this recipe one day in advance.

Makes approximately 10 pies

For the pastry
275g/10oz plain flour
150g/5oz margarine
1 egg, beaten
enough cold water to bind the dough
pinch of salt and pepper

Sieve the flour and salt and pepper into a mixing bowl. Rub in the margarine with your fingertips until the mixture resembles fine breadcrumbs. Mix in the beaten egg with a knife, followed by the cold water, a little at a time, until the mixture forms a dough. Cover with clingfilm and place in the fridge until needed.

For the skirts and kidney
450g/1lb skirts
1 kidney (some people prefer to use only ½ a kidney)
a little oil for frying
1 onion, chopped
2 cloves of garlic, crushed
½ tsp ground cumin
½ tsp ground coriander
1½ tsp tomato purée
300ml/½ pint chicken stock

Cut the skirts into bite-sized pieces with a kitchen scissors (a scissors seems to work better than a knife in this case). With a knife, chop the kidney into small pieces also.

In a little oil, fry the onion and garlic for a couple of minutes, then add skirts and kidneys quickly followed by the cumin, coriander and tomato purée. Stir well and allow to cook until all the meat is sealed, then add the chicken stock. Bring the pot to the boil and then reduce to a simmer, cover the pot with a tight-fitting lid and continue to cook for 2½–3 hours.

When the skirts are cooked, they should have a very tender, yet 'pleasantly' stringy texture. Leave the mixture to cool.

Preheat the oven to 180°C/355°F/gas mark 4. Lightly grease a muffin or Yorkshire pudding tin (like a queen cake tin but with larger moulds). On a well-floured surface, roll out the pastry and line the bottom and sides of the moulds with pastry. Use more than you think you might need – the pastry should come well up over the sides. You can trim it later. Put a dessert spoonful of the skirt and kidney mixture on to each piece of pastry in the moulds, brush the edges with a little beaten egg and cover the top with more pastry.

Trim the sides and seal both edges of the pie with a fork so that the filling cannot escape. Cut a little hole in the top of the pie with the tip of a sharp knife (so that steam can escape) and brush the pies with beaten egg.

Place in the centre of the oven and cook for 20–30 minutes. Enjoy hot or cold.

Put more of the meat mixture than juice/gravy into the pie, otherwise the pie will become too soggy. You can always heat the leftover gravy and serve it in a jug on the side if people would like more.

Pauline's Two-Minute Marinade

A quick and very tasty marinade suitable for spare ribs, chicken wings and sausages.
This simple marinade turns any ordinary dish into an unforgettable feast.

In a bowl mix:

2 tbsp sugar

3 tbsp oil

3 tbsp soy sauce

3 tbsp tomato ketchup

2 garlic cloves, crushed, or 1 tsp garlic salt

When all the ingredients have been well mixed, pour on to the ribs.

Kathleen Noonan's Original Recipe for Bodice with Cabbage or Turnip

This is a recipe taken from the late Kathleen Noonan's recipe notebook. Her daughter, Pauline, is proud to pass this recipe on. This recipe would have been widely used from the 1940s to the 1970s in Cork.

Serves 3–4 people

2 racks of bodice

1 head of cabbage or 1 turnip

Cut the bodice into pieces and cover with cold water. Bring the pot to the boil and then simmer for 1½ hours. Remove the bodice from the pot when it is cooked and boil your cabbage and turnip in the same water.

Serve with mashed potatoes.

Crúbeen, Parsley and Thyme Potato Cakes

Great served as a starter or a snack with drinks. And discussing the main ingredient ensures that the conversation keeps on flowing!

Makes 8–10 cakes

2 crúbeens (cooked as in Kathleen's recipe), with the meat and fat removed
   and chopped finely, see below
50g/2oz plain flour
450g/1lb potatoes, boiled and mashed
1 egg, beaten
2 scallions, finely chopped
1 tsp chopped thyme
handful chopped parsley
salt and pepper
milk if needed
flour for shaping
a little butter and oil for frying

In a large bowl, mix all the ingredients together. If the mixture is not binding properly, add a little milk. Using a small amount of flour on your hands, shape the mixture into small balls and then firm them down with the palm of your hand to make a cake shape. You should get 8–10 cakes from this mixture.

Heat a little oil and butter in a frying pan and fry the cakes on both sides until golden. Serve immediately.

About a Good Knife

Rory Conner is a professional cutler. He designs and makes knives at his home in West Cork. His work has received many awards and accolades for his master craftsmanship. Rory designs and makes a wide range of knives, including kitchen knives, table cutlery, carving sets and cheese knives. He also designs and makes a range of knives for outdoor pursuits such as hunting, fishing, sailing and camping and specialised knives for gardening and various crafts. He will also work closely with clients who wish to commission a one-off knife.

Rory works in stainless steel and carbon steel for the blades but Damas steel is used for a patterned finish. Handle materials include bog oak, ethically sourced exotic hardwoods, stag horn and coloured wood laminates. The result of Rory's unique talent is a truly beautiful work of art, which may also be used and enjoyed for a lifetime.

All Rory's knives come with a lifetime guarantee.

People always ask me, 'what makes a good knife?' That is a difficult question to answer, but I believe a good knife is the knife that you like to use for most jobs. Knives are the basic tool for kitchen work and having a couple that you enjoy using makes cooking even more satisfying.

There are kitchen knives for every culinary purpose, but most of us will probably only use three at the most. These are:
- A small short-bladed knife for peeling, called a peeler.
- A broad triangular-bladed knife for preparing vegetables, called a chef's knife.
- A long narrow-bladed knife for boning meat, called a boning knife. This is useful but not essential.

It is worth buying good-quality knives which will be durable, will stay sharp and which you will enjoy using. Most knives these days are made from stainless steel, which does not stain or rust easily and will keep a keen edge for a long time.

Older knives tend to be made from carbon steel. It is softer than stainless steel,

Boning Knife

Chef's Knife

Peeler Knife

Vegetable Knife

RORY CONNER
Handmade Knives

Oyster Knife

making it easier to re-sharpen. The blades on these knives tend to stain easily and have a dark patina. Some chefs love this steel and still use these knives. The type of steel you decide on is a personal choice, as both are equally good.

The handles of knives can be made from metal, wood laminate, wood or plastic and all of these materials have their own qualities and work well in use. The handles are attached to the blade with rivets or by forming directly around the steel tang.

When you are buying a knife, examine the back of the blade to see if it is straight. Blades that are slightly bent indicate poor quality control in the production.

Ice-hardening or sub-zero quench contributes to the quality of the steel, and this will result in a knife that maintains a good edge. Ice-hardening is achieved by a cryogenic (vacuum ice-hardening) process which cools the steel very quickly; the steel is then tempered in a gasless chamber, which preserves flexibility whilst giving the knife optimal hardness and durability values. You may pay more for this, but it's worth it.

Turn the knife over and look at the cutting edge, which should be almost invisible; if you can see the cutting edge in places then the knife is blunt.

The handle, regardless of material, should be smooth with no sharp corners. The balance should be right for you and should not feel heavy in your hand. The knife should move easily as you move your hand and should feel comfortable to hold.

Look after your knives well and do not put them in the dishwasher. Sharpen little and often, just before you use the knife. If you use a knife steel for sharpening your knives, wash it in boiling water and soap to improve its sharpening ability.

Knives should be stored in a block or rack, well out of the reach of children. If you are storing carbon steel knives, it's a good idea to oil the blades with vegetable oil and wrap in clingfilm.

It is more useful to have one good knife that you like to use than several average knives. My advice is to invest in one good knife and add to this over time. Treat your knives well and they should give you years of good service and happy cooking.

Rory Conner

Mr Bell

Stalls 15, 25 & 26

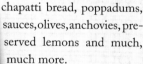

riss Belamajoub moved to Cork from his native Morocco in the early 1970s. He had trained and worked as a chef for several years but in the mid-1970s he decided to start up his own business. He opened a small shop selling ethnic clothing and crafts in the Winthrop Arcade and the business prospered for several years. However, in the early 1980s ethnic clothing went out of fashion and Driss decided to diversify into foods and spices which were fairly impossible to source in Cork at the time. As he frequently travelled back and forth to Morocco and always brought couscous and spices back with him, he decided to bring a little more – just enough to stock a small shop in the English Market. Spices and curries were not yet popular in early 1980s Cork, but slowly people's tastes changed as they became more widely travelled. Today Mr Bell has two stalls selling everything from earthenware tagines to herbs, spices, noodles and rices, chapatti bread, poppadums, sauces, olives, anchovies, preserved lemons and much, much more.

Royal Korma Mr Bell Style

A delicious, authentic, aromatic korma. What could be nicer? A great dish to serve when having friends around after work. You can easily prepare this recipe a day in advance and all you have to do is reheat it and cook the rice before your guests arrive.

Serves 6

500g/1lb very lean lamb or chicken, cubed	4 green cardamom pods
2 onions	400mls/16fl oz coconut milk
6 garlic cloves	1 tsp sugar
1 small piece of ginger	1 tsp poppy seeds, ground
½ tsp chilli powder	3 tsp ground almonds
1 tsp coriander powder	a pinch of saffron
1 tsp cumin powder	salt and freshly ground black pepper

Finely grate 1 onion, the garlic and ginger until it resembles a smooth paste. Slice the remaining onion thinly and fry on a medium heat until golden.

Add the garlic, onion and ginger paste to the saucepan, cook for a minute or two and then add the chilli, coriander and cumin powders. Fry on a medium heat for 3–4 minutes.

Next add the meat and the green cardamom pods to the saucepan and cook until the meat is sealed. Then, add the coconut milk and sugar to the pan and simmer, covered, on a low heat until the meat is tender. Add the poppy seeds to the pan and continue to cook until the sauce has thickened. Finally, season well with salt and black pepper, sprinkle the ground almonds and saffron over the dish, stir in well and cook for a further 5 minutes.

Serve with basmati rice.

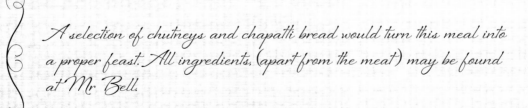

A selection of chutneys and chapatti bread would turn this meal into a proper feast. All ingredients, (apart from the meat) may be found at Mr Bell.

Mr Bell's Green Curry

A taste of Thailand on a plate. Subtle curry and spice flavours mingle to form an unforgettably delicious dish.

Serves 4–6

3 tbsp green curry paste
1 tbsp Irish rapeseed oil
1 400ml tin coconut milk
400g/14oz diced beef, chicken, or whole prawns
2 kaffir lime leaves
1½ tbsp palm sugar
1½ tbsp fish sauce
2 small aubergines, quartered
2–3 red chillies without the seeds, sliced diagonally
1 tbsp sweet basil leaves
sweet basil leaves and red chillies to garnish
salt and black pepper to season

Sauté the curry paste in a little oil over a medium heat until fragrant. Reduce the heat and slowly stir in half of the coconut milk, a little at a time, until a film of green oil comes to the surface.

Add the meat, chicken or prawns and the kaffir lime leaves and continue to cook until the curry begins to bubble, then add the remaining coconut, milk, sugar and the fish sauce. Simmer until the meat is cooked through, then bring the saucepan back up to the boil again.

As soon as the curry returns to the boil, add the aubergines. Cook for a further 10–15 minutes then sprinkle with the sweet basil leaves and chopped chillies, and season well with salt and black pepper. Turn off the heat, arrange the curry on a serving dish and garnish with more sweet basil leaves and red chillies before serving with jasmine rice.

Mr Bell's Orange Blossom Cake with Cardamom

Perfect with a cup of coffee as a mid-morning treat or equally good as a dessert.

Serves 8–12

150g/5oz butter, softened

200g/7oz caster sugar

juice and zest of 1 orange

4 large free-range eggs, beaten

150g/5oz self-raising flour

125g/4 ½oz ground almonds

1 tsp baking powder

4 tbsp orange marmalade mixed with 2 tsp boiling water

For the orange syrup

85g/3½oz caster sugar

juice of 3 oranges

1½ tsp orange blossom water

For decoration

100g/4oz caster sugar

6–8 cardamom pods

1 large orange, sliced very thinly

50g/2oz shelled unsalted pistachios

You will need an 8"/20cm round springform cake tin, greased and lined

Heat the oven to 160°C/320°F/gas mark 3. Cream the butter and sugar together. Add the juice and zest of the orange, and beat into the mixture. Fold in the flour, almonds and baking powder until the mixture becomes smooth and creamy. Transfer to the cake tin, then drizzle the orange marmalade over the top of the cake and drag it into the mixture using a knife. Make sure the marmalade is covered by the cake mixture, or it will burn. Bake in the middle of the oven for about 20 minutes, then cover the cake with tin foil so it won't burn. Continue cooking for another 30 minutes.

For the syrup

Heat the sugar, orange juice and orange blossom water until the sugar has dissolved. When the cake is cooked, prick it with a skewer and pour the syrup over it. Then allow the cake to cool completely in the tin. Run a knife around the edges of the tin to help release the cake with ease. Transfer to a cake stand or serving plate.

To decorate, place the sugar in a pan with the cardamom pods and 100ml/4fl oz boiling water. Heat gently until the sugar dissolves, add the orange slices and pistachios and allow the flavours to infuse over a low heat. Finally, remove the orange slices, pistachios and cardamom pods and arrange in the centre of the cake.

Serve with a little Greek yoghurt and a drizzle of honey.

The Joys of Tea and Cakes

Tea. Even the word is soothing, placating, reassuring. Tea, 'a drink with jam and bread'. Tea, a warming amber liquid made from leaves and boiling water. Tea. A brew. A break. A remedy. A drink taken at breakfast, in the afternoon and at 'tea time'. Where would we be without our beloved tea? Its ritual preparation and consumption punctuates our days with mini-meditations, philosophical musings, theories and resolutions.

The offering of tea to a visitor, guest, friend or acquaintance displays hospitality, kindness and a warm welcome. It's just plain good manners really. But there is also so much more to a cup of tea than meets the eye. 'Tea' can be a codeword for so many things that we might be otherwise too timid to say. I care about you. I'm worried about you. Let's talk. Let's call a truce. I have some great news! I have some very bad news.

For the Irish especially, the offering of tea can have several different meanings.

'Would you like a cup of tea?': I like you. I have time for you, and I would like to spend time with you.

'Are you sure you won't have a cup of tea?': I hope you don't mean to tell me that you're rejecting my hospitality and you're going to turn around and leave without bidding me the time of day!

'Well, I'm putting the kettle on anyway': You'll sit down there and you'll have a cup of tea whether you want one or not.

Mrs Doyle from Dermot Morgan's wonderful comedy television series springs to mind. *Father Ted*, a series about a Catholic priest, the church in Ireland, his housekeeper and . . . . tea. To refuse a cup of tea from the pot of Mrs Doyle was to commit a very, very serious social gaffe indeed.

Jane Austen frequently made reference to the preparation of tea, the drinking of tea, the joy and anticipation experienced in preparing a pot of tea. Jane was the 'tea maker' and 'tea keeper' in her family. A sort of Mistress of Tea Ceremonies. She frequently made reference in her books to taking tea in the morning for breakfast, in the afternoon as a pick-me-up, tea at the ball as a refreshment and tea last thing at night before going to bed. Her day was punctuated with the taking of tea. And of course, as sharing a pot of tea in female company is usually the preamble to a good 'chat', perhaps the suspense of what might be divulged over the china cups was as titillating to Jane as the tea itself. As Shakespeare so aptly put it: 'There's many a slip, twixt cup and lip.' This would have been typical Jane Austen territory.

Tea, of course, originally came from China, invented in 2750BC after the leaves of *Camellia sinensis* accidentally fell into a bowl of hot water in front of the Emperor Shen Nung. He liked the smell and so poured himself the world's first cup of tea.

In Europe, we were a little slower to catch on. Our first tea came from Holland in 1650 and was initially referred to as 'tay', which indeed the Irish still refer to it as.

The Japanese have long recognised the importance of the taking of tea and make a formal ceremony of it. In Ireland, we may not afford much importance to our tea-making but, nevertheless, we should not underestimate the significance of the 'ceremony' in our own little kitchens. A simple tea bag, a favourite cup, the 'dunkability' of a biscuit, are all very important factors in our day-to-day dalliance with tea.

But, however simple and enjoyable the solitary cuppa can be, there is nothing so superb, so joyous and uplifting, as tea and cakes with company. Conversation flows easily, no social one-upmanship is called for, it's just a friendly chat over a nice cup of tea and delicious cake.

In the course of compiling this book, I dreamt one night of a table covered in cakes and dainties, teapots and china cups. Cakes oozing with cream and jams and dripping with sticky icing. Tea steaming from silver teapots, quivering in fine china cups. The dream was so clear and tangible that it stayed with me all of the next day. Could I re-create this wonderful scene to share with readers?

But time was running out. The manuscript was due to be sent to the publishers. I would have to abandon my dream. Or would I?

Inspiration came in a flash over a mug of tea and a spiced beef sandwich. What if I placed an advertisement in the local parish newsletter and asked for volunteers to take part in a 'Recipe Book Baking Bonanza'? No sooner had the advert appeared than my phone began to ring. The date was set, the cakes were baked, and on a crisp January morning a convoy of cars arrived at my house and, one after another, my fellow tea and cake enthusiasts all piled into my kitchen. An army of bakers all bearing cakes!

The table was set with the best china, the silver teapot received a last-minute buff, the cakes were all laid upon the table and photographed. A close-up of the coffee cake, a side view of the muffins, the Victoria sandwich in the background, tea in china cups. The dream had indeed become a reality. When the photographer had finished, we enjoyed a nice cup of tea and sampled all the cakes. What a joy it was, that day of tea and cakes.

Very special thanks to Margaret Mullarkey, Tricia O'Donovan, Siobhán Kelly, Grace Gallagher, mother and son team Finola Stephens and Diarmuid Hurley and Niamh Dennehy.

You can admire their beautiful cakes in the accompanying photographs.

Finola and Diarmuid's Lemon Cupcakes

Beautiful and delicious cupcakes, the perfect treat to enjoy with friends.

Makes 12 cupcakes

For the cakes
125g/4oz soft margarine, at room temperature
125g/4oz caster sugar
150g/5oz plain flour, sieved with ½ tsp baking powder
grated zest of ½ lemon
2 large eggs, beaten

For the icing
75g/3oz unsalted butter,
    at room temperature
175g/6oz icing sugar, sieved
grated zest of ½ lemon
2 tsp squeezed lemon juice
a couple of drops of yellow food colouring

You will also need
fairy-cake tin
paper cases
piping set
decorations for icing

Preheat the oven to 180°C/350°F/gas mark 4. First put the paper cases into the cake tin. Next, cream the margarine in a large bowl. Add the sugar and lemon zest and continue to cream until light and fluffy. Add the beaten egg slowly and mix thoroughly.

Fold in the sieved flour and baking powder. Place spoonfuls of the mixture into paper cases and place in the preheated oven. Bake for 10–12 minutes until risen and golden. Turn cakes out on to a rack and leave to cool.

For the icing, cream the unsalted butter in a bowl. Gradually beat in the icing sugar, lemon zest, food colouring and enough lemon juice to get a consistency suitable for piping. Pipe the icing on to the cooled cakes using a small rose nozzle. Decorate.

Grace's Victoria Sponge with Mascarpone and Strawberries

Serves 12

225g/8oz butter, softened
225g/8oz caster sugar
4 large eggs
1 tsp vanilla extract
½ tsp salt
225g/8oz self-raising flour

For the icing
250g/9oz mascarpone or freshly whipped cream
1 tsp vanilla paste or extract
2 tbsp icing sugar, plus extra to dust
6–7 tbsp good raspberry jam
250g/9oz fresh strawberries or raspberries

You will need two 8-inch sandwich tins, lightly oiled and lined at the base. Heat the oven to 180°C/350°F/gas mark 4. Cream the butter and sugar together until light and fluffy. Beat in the eggs, stir through the vanilla extract, then fold in the flour and the salt until you have a smooth batter. Divide equally between the two tins and bake for 25 to 30 minutes, until a skewer inserted in the middle comes out clean. Remove from the oven and cool on a wire rack.

To make the filling, whisk the mascarpone, vanilla and icing sugar until smooth. Be careful not to overwhisk. Place one cooled cake upside down on a serving plate and spread the raspberry jam over the top. Top with mascarpone and fresh raspberries. Top with the other cake, right side up. Dust with icing sugar and serve.

Niamh's Lemon and Lime Drizzle Cake

Enjoy this delicious cake with a cup of Earl Grey tea.

Serves 10–12

180g/6oz butter
200g/7oz caster sugar
finely grated rind of 1 lemon
2 eggs
200g/7oz self-raising flour
125ml/4fl oz of buttermilk

Syrup
120g/4oz icing sugar
50ml/2fl oz fresh lemon juice

Icing
200g/7oz icing sugar
3 tbsp boiling water
juice of ½ a lime

To decorate
Grated rind of 1 lemon and 1 lime

Grease and line a 450g/1lb cake tin. Preheat your oven to 180°C/355°F/gas mark 4. Cream the butter and sugar together until pale in colour and creamy. Sift in a little flour and beat into the mixture. Next add a little buttermilk and beaten egg and, once again, beat in well. Alternate like this between the flour and the milk and beaten eggs (mixing after each addition) until all the ingredients have been added. Bake in the centre of the oven for 40–45 minutes.

When the cake has cooled, make perforations with a skewer all along the cake. Heat the syrup ingredients in a saucepan, until the mixture resembles a syrup, then pour it all over the cake – it should soak into the perforations you have made.

Finally, to make the icing, mix the icing sugar and boiling water and lime juice together and pour over the cake – the icing should run down the sides of the cake. Decorate with the grated rind of the lemon and lime.

Margaret's Butterfly Cakes

Dainty and charming, this much-loved recipe never goes out of fashion.

Makes 10–12 cakes

225g/8oz self-raising flour
125g/4oz butter
50g/2oz caster sugar
1 large fresh egg
1tsp baking powder

For the filling
1tsp whipped cream per cake
½ tsp strawberry jam per cake

Mix the sugar and butter to a fluffy creamy white consistency. Add the beaten egg, a little at a time. Add the flour two tablespoons at a time, folding the flour into the mixture after each addition. When the flour has all been incorporated, the mixture should have a nice dropping consistency (i.e. it should drop easily off a spoon). Finally, spoon the mixture into paper cases (in a muffin tin) and bake for 15 minutes 180°C/355°F/gas mark 4.

Leave the cakes to cool on a wire tray. When they are completely cool, slice off the top and cut this piece in half to form the wings. Place a ½ teaspoon of jam on top of the cake, followed by a spoon of whipped cream. Place the two halves of sponge cut from the top of the cake onto the cream to resemble butterfly wings.

Niamh's Coffee Cake

A classic coffee cake with a hint of apricot.

Serves 10–12

200g/7oz unsalted butter
200g/7oz brown sugar
3 large eggs
1 tsp of instant espresso powder mixed with a little boiling water
or
2 tsp of Irel coffee essence
or
3 tbsp of freshly brewed espresso coffee
200g/7oz self-raising flour
1 tsp baking powder

For the icing
150g/5oz unsalted butter
250g/9oz icing sugar
2 tbsp espresso coffee
or
2 tsp Irel coffee essence
or
2 tsp of instant espresso powder
   mixed with a little boiling water

For the filling and to decorate
3 tbsp apricot jam
50g/2oz flaked almonds, lightly toasted (you can toast them in
   the oven on a baking tray for 5 minutes)

Preheat the oven to 180°C/355°F/gas mark 4. Grease and line two 8 inch sandwich tins. Beat together the butter and sugar in a large bowl until pale and fluffy, then beat in the eggs, one at a time. Sift the flour into the mixture and fold in. Fold in the coffee. Divide between the two sandwich tins and spread out evenly. Bake for 20–25 minutes until golden and the sponge springs back when pressed gently with your fingertips. Turn out on to a wire rack to cool.

Beat the butter, icing sugar and coffee together until all the ingredients have combined well (2–3 minutes of beating).

To assemble, spread one half of the sponge sandwich with the apricot jam, spread the other with 3–4 tablespoons of the icing and sandwich both cakes together. Cover the entire cake with the remainder of the icing, smoothing with a palette knife. Press the toasted almonds on to the side of the cake and decorate the top of the cake with the walnuts.

Tricia's Savoury and Sweet Scones

This classic scone recipe is a lifesaver when you need to come up with something special at short notice. Who doesn't love a freshly baked scone? Serve the savoury scones with Irish stew or a bowl of soup for something a little out of the ordinary.

Makes 10–12 scones

225g/9oz plain flour
4 tsp baking powder
¼ tsp salt
50g/2oz butter
150ml/5fl oz milk
1 medium egg
1 small red onion, chopped and fried in a little butter
2 tsp chopped thyme
50g/2oz grated cheese may also be used (optional)

Preheat the oven to 210°C/410°F/gas mark 6 and lightly grease a baking tray. Sift the flour, baking powder and salt into a bowl and rub in the butter, until the mixture resembles breadcrumbs. Stir in the onion and thyme or the grated cheese – use both if you like! Finally, add the milk and mix lightly into a soft dough.

Roll the dough out to 1.25cm/½" thickness and cut into rounds. Place on the greased baking tray. Brush the tops with beaten egg and bake for 10–12 minutes or until golden brown. Cool on a wire rack.

Sweet Scones

Follow the above recipe, leaving out the onion, thyme and/or cheese (of course) and add 50g/2oz of caster sugar, which will produce a sweet-tasting scone. You can also add a handful of sultanas or raisins or even chopped cherries, apple and walnuts.

Siobhán's Strawberries and Cream Cupcakes

Creamy, dreamy and heavenly cupcakes.

Makes 10–12 cupcakes

175g/6oz butter, softened or soft margarine
175g/6oz caster sugar
3 large eggs, beaten
175g/6oz self-raising flour, sieved
1 tsp vanilla extract

Vanilla buttercream
275g/10oz icing sugar, sieved
150g/5oz butter, softened
1 tsp vanilla extract
3 tbsp milk
pink concentrated gel colouring
slices of strawberry for decoration

Preheat oven to 180°C/355°F/gas mark 4. Line a 12-hole muffin tin with paper cases. Cream the butter and sugar together until light and fluffy. Add the vanilla and beat in alternate tablespoons of flour and egg until the mixture is pale and smooth. Divide the mixture between the 12 cases and bake on the middle shelf of the oven for approximately 20 minutes or until well-risen and golden brown. Cool the cakes on a wire rack.

To make the buttercream icing, cream the butter, icing sugar and vanilla extract together. Add the milk gradually, if the icing seems a little dry. Cream until a smooth icing is formed. Add a very small amount of colouring at a time (using the tip of a cocktail stick) until the desired colour is achieved.

Fill your piping bag with icing (fitted with a large rosette piping nozzle) and pipe swirls of buttercream on top of the cupcakes. Add a slice of strawberry to complete the decoration.

McDonnells

Stall P4

Paddy McDonnell has stood in the same spot in the market for over 60 years. He took over the running of the stall from his mother Bridget McDonnell, whom Paddy describes as 'an extremely hard-working and wonderful mother of nine children'. Paddy was the eldest. He now describes himself as semi-retired and his motto is 'Tóg go bóg é' (take it easy).

Paddy says, 'When I was a young boy, onions were always used to add flavour to everything because they were cheap and easy to come by, or even grow if you had a little garden. The women used to put them into all the everyday dishes, from tripe and drisheen, to skirts and kidneys and bodice. They didn't even bother to cut them; they just peeled them and in they went to the pot, whole. They were seen as having great medicinal properties, from helping to shift a cough or cold to settling an upset tummy. Sometimes they were studded with cloves and boiled in milk with lots of white pepper for particularly bad cases. My mother always used to say that onions were the 'scavenger of the stomach'. The onion was always cere-

moniously fished out of the pot at the end of serving and given to whomever at the table was in most need of medicinal attention, or whoever was entitled to a treat that day. If it's flavour you're after, then you can't beat an onion.'

Paddy's Irish Onion Soup with Fried Bread

Serves 4–6

6 large onions or 8 medium, thinly sliced
Irish rapeseed oil
1 tsp of sugar
3 cloves of garlic, crushed or very finely chopped
600mls/1 pint of beef stock
300mls/½ pint white wine
1 bay leaf
2 sprigs of thyme
salt and pepper
1 fresh loaf of bread
butter for buttering the slices of bread
20g/¾ oz Gabriel cheese

In a large saucepan, sauté the onions in the oil on a medium to high heat until well browned. You will need to stir them occasionally to stop them from burning. You do want them to take on a colour though, so cooking them at a low heat won't do. Add the sugar after about 10 minutes of cooking, which will help with the caramelisation process, and then continue cooking the onions for 20–30 minutes after that. Then add the garlic and cook for a minute or two.

Add the stock, wine, bay leaf and thyme. Partially cover the saucepan and cook for another 30 minutes. Season with salt and pepper. Remove the bay leaf and thyme.

Pop a small chunk of Gabriel cheese into the bottom of four to six warmed bowls and ladle the soup over the top. The cheese will melt into the soup.

For the fried bread

Butter as many slices of bread as you wish to fry. Heat a frying pan on a medium heat and drizzle in a little oil. Fry each slice for 2–3 minutes per side or until just golden brown. If you are the kind of person who keeps reserved bacon fat in your fridge, then add a knob of this also to the frying pan for a really naughty treat, otherwise just stick with the 'healthier' version of the recipe!

Apple Cake

Apple cake is a firm favourite in most Irish homes, even though recipes can vary greatly. The basis for this delicious cake is always the same – cooking apples and sponge cake mixture. Enjoy hot (served with cream or ice-cream) or cold with a nice cup of tea. One slice is never enough.

Serves 10–12

50g/2oz Irish butter
128g/4½ oz sugar
1 egg, beaten
4 cooking apples, peeled, cored and diced
1 tsp vanilla essence
125g/4oz plain flour
½ tsp cinnamon
½ tsp salt
½ tsp bicarbonate of soda
½ tsp baking powder
32g (a small handful) of chopped walnuts, optional

Preheat the oven to 180°C/355°F/gas mark 4. Prepare a 20cm square cake pan by greasing it well. In a large bowl, cream the butter and sugar together until light and fluffy. Add in the eggs and beat well for a minute or two. Add the apples and vanilla and stir well. Next, sift in the dry ingredients and mix well.

Pour the batter into the cake tin and bake until the cake is lightly browned, after about 45 minutes. Test by inserting a skewer into the centre of the cake – if it comes out clean, then the cake is cooked. Allow the cake to cool for 10–15 minutes in the tin and then remove it and serve hot with whipped cream or vanilla ice-cream.

Bubble Brothers

Stall 4C

Bubble Brothers began supplying quality wines in Cork in the late 1990s and subsequently took a stall in the English Market. Originally founded by Billy Forrester, Billy and his team of trusty wine savants quickly established themselves as dependable and scholarly in their knowledge of wines. Bubble Brothers supply original champagnes and wines from around the world, plum wine and related drinks, coffee and one or two specialist beers. Their shop in the English Market is one of the few places in the country to offer a choice of some of the finest cigars in the world. When you visit the Bubble Brothers stall at the English Market, you have access to your very own personal sommelier. Every customer is given undivided attention and advice when choosing.

Bubble Brothers has become synonymous in Cork with the highest quality and value and their eclectic mix of all things 'masterly' – Japanese 'shots', Cuban cigars and superb coffee from Cork Coffee Roasters – have made them a must-visit venue in the English Market. Bubble Brothers also run bespoke wine tastings and their website (www.bubble brothers.com) is well worth a visit, if only to read the blog – which is always very entertaining.

Bubble Brothers' Champagne Jelly with Strawberries

Billy says: 'Don't panic! We don't expect you to use "real" Champagne for this. You can cheat and use Cava, Prosecco or any "New World" sparkling wine. This dessert is very easy to make, will impress your guests no end and is a great finale to any special meal.'

Serves 4

4 leaves gelatine
300ml/½ pint sparkling wine of your choice
2 tsp caster sugar
8 strawberries cut into quarters

Place the gelatine leaves in a bowl of cold water for 5 minutes or until soft. Squeeze the leaves like a sponge and discard the water. Put 100ml/3½ fl oz of the sparkling wine in a bowl that fits snugly over a pan of boiling water, add the gelatine and sugar and heat gently until the gelatine has dissolved. Then remove from the heat, add the remaining sparkling wine and pour into a jug.

Place 2 strawberries, quartered, in the bottom of each glass (champagne glasses if possible). Pour over just enough of the jelly mixture to cover the strawberries and refrigerate until set. When the jelly has set over the strawberries, pour in the remaining jelly. Do this very carefully and slowly, otherwise your unset jelly will penetrate the set layer of jelly and the end result could look a bit messy. Refrigerate until set.

Red Wine Jus

This is the perfect sauce to serve with any good-quality red meat dish.
It is also known as red wine reduction.

Serves 6–8*

A little oil for frying
2 shallots, chopped
175ml/6fl oz port
175ml/6fl oz red wine
1 sprig of fresh rosemary
1 bay leaf
750ml/1¼ pints homemade beef stock
2 tsp butter
salt and pepper to taste

Put a little oil in the saucepan, add the shallots and cook until light brown. Add the port, red wine and herbs and bring to the boil. Simmer and reduce by half. Add stock, simmer and reduce by half. Season to taste.

Strain the jus through a fine sieve. Return to the heat and bring to the boil, then melt in the butter, stir well and serve.

*Any leftover jus can be frozen and reused later.

Supreme Chicken Surprise

A decadent but delicious dish to share with friends or family for a special occasion.

Serves 4, or 2 very hungry people

A pack of ready-made puff pastry, thawed if frozen
1 egg, beaten
butter and olive oil
2 good-quality skinless chicken breast fillets
8 button mushrooms
1 bottle dessert wine, perhaps a Brightwater Nelson Riesling
1 chicken stock cube
1 small carton of single cream
small bunch of seedless green grapes

Optional for the deluxe version: 4 fresh large scallops

Preheat the oven to 200°C/390°F/gas mark 6. Roll the pastry to 1cm/¼ inch in thickness if not using pre-rolled sheets. Put a small bowl on the pastry and cut around it to make four disc shapes. Brush each disc with egg and place on a buttered flat baking tray. Bake for about 20 minutes or until golden and risen.

In a large non-stick pan, gently melt a knob of butter and a dash of oil. Add the chicken breast cut in 3cm/1 inch cubes and cook on a moderate heat. Add the mushrooms after 10 minutes and cook for a further 5 minutes. Add the wine and stock cube and simmer fast until reduced by half. Lower the heat and add the cream. Add at least 8 grapes, cut in half. If using the scallops, add these last. Do not overcook the scallops; 1–2 minutes should suffice.

Serve on hot plates and place a disc of pastry on top. Accompany with small new buttered spuds and steamed broccoli, or garden peas and carrots.

A good wine to serve would be a matching Brightwater Nelson Riesling or perhaps a 4 Chemins Côtes du Rhône Villages, or a Laudun Sols et Sens Blanc.

Spring Rosé Pork Steak

A quirky marriage of savoury and sweet flavours. Discussing the ingredients alone is guaranteed to keep the conversation flowing at the dinner table.

1 pork steak fillet, trimmed (ask your butcher)
a little butter and olive oil
1 bottle of Mas Codina Pendés Rosé
3cm/1 inch cube of peeled fresh ginger, or ½ teaspoon of ginger powder
8–10 semi-dried apricots
cornflour for thickening
1 medium leek, trimmed and cleaned
1 large or 2 small fresh peaches
a little honey
a dash of tomato ketchup
a red rose for garnish, washed (the petals are good to eat!)

Slice the pork in 2cm/½ inch slices and gently fry in a little butter and olive oil in a large deep pan. Add finely chopped ginger or ginger powder.

Slice leek thinly and add when the pork has begun to brown a little. Fry gently for a few minutes. Add most of the Pendés Rosé and turn up the heat to reduce. Reserve a little and mix with cornflour to thicken a few moments before serving. Add a dash of honey, a splash of tomato ketchup and the apricots. Turn down to a gentle simmer and cook for no more than 30 minutes.

Meanwhile cook one small cup of basmati rice per person. Measure out the rice in cups and add twice the amount in water (for example, 4 cups of rice will need to be cooked in 8 cups of water). Add a little salt to the water. Bring the rice to the boil, put on a tight lid and turn down to simmer as soon as it boils. Turn off the heat after 20 minutes and leave on the lid.

Slice and stone the peach. Pull the petals off the rose and rinse and pat dry. Serve rice on hot plates, make a well and spoon the rosé pork into the middle. Sprinkle with petals and slices of peach.

Serve a sparkling wine, well chilled, with the meal.

Coffee Central

Stall 27

C offee Central is a favourite refuelling pit stop in the heart of the market. It is popular with customers and traders alike. Mary Rose Daly serves coffee with a smile at the stall where her father, John Rose, previously sold pork and bacon for 30 years. The Rose family come from a strong grocery retailing background in Cork city dating back to the 1940s. In 2001 Mary decided to embrace the unquenchable twenty-first century desire for the coffee bean and converted her pork and bacon stall into a coffee shop. She hasn't looked back since. This is Mary's recipe for Irish coffee.

Irish Coffee

The head chef Joseph Sheridan is widely believed to be the man who 'invented' Irish coffee in the 1940s. A group of travel-weary Americans disembarked from a Pan Am flying boat at Foynes one wild and wet winter's evening. Sheridan decided to add whiskey to their coffee to help warm them up. When they asked him if it was a Brazilian coffee that he had served, he told them no, it was 'an Irish coffee!'

Makes 1 coffee

30ml/1tbsp Irish whiskey
1 tsp brown sugar
175ml/6fl oz freshly brewed coffee
1 generous tbsp lightly whipped cream

Pour the whiskey into an Irish coffee glass or a glass with a stem, add the sugar, stir and dissolve. Leave the teaspoon in the glass (it helps to conduct the heat and prevents the glass from cracking) and pour in the freshly brewed coffee. Stir well and remove the spoon. Dip a tablespoon in a little bowl of boiling water and then spoon up the cream. The warmed spoon will ensure that the cream glides smoothly off the spoon and sits proudly on top of the coffee without mixing into the coffee.

Serve at the end of a good meal, or even as 'dessert'.

Irish Coffee Cupcakes

A delicious little cupcake recipe. Perfect for a mid-morning treat with an Americano or Cappuccino.

Makes about 12 cupcakes

For the cupcakes
175g/6oz butter, at room temperature
175g/6oz caster sugar
1 teaspoon instant espresso powder dissolved in 2 tbsp boiling water
3 large eggs
175g/6oz self-raising flour

For the frosting
360mls/16fl oz double cream
1 tbsp icing sugar
1 tbsp Irish whiskey
instant espresso powder for dusting

Preheat the oven to 180°C/355°F/gas mark 4. Line the muffin tin with muffin cases. Cream the butter and sugar until light and fluffy. Add the coffee essence or instant coffee mixture (cooled), and beat in the flour and eggs, a little at a time, until everything has been incorporated.

Fill the muffin moulds three-quarters full with the mixture. Bake for about 15–20 minutes (or until a skewer comes out clean when inserted into the centre of a muffin). Leave to cool and then turn out from the cupcake tins.

To make the frosting, whisk together the cream and icing sugar until medium peaks form. Add the whiskey and whisk until stiffer peaks form.

Top each cupcake with the frosting. Use a piping bag if you have one and dust with espresso powder to finish.

The
Roughty Fruit King

Stall 20

The Roughty Fruit King originally started out as a fruit and vegetable stall but diversified along the way. The stall first opened in 1961, when Michael F. Murphy and his new bride Peggy decided to start their own business by taking a vacant stall in the English Market. 'People always ask where the name of the stall comes from,' says Garrett, the couple's son, who now helps to run the stall. 'It is called after the river Roughty that flows near my mother's home-place in Kilgarvan, County Kerry. Mum and Dad were truly devoted to one another; theirs was a great love story.'

In 2010 Michael F. Murphy retired from his stall due to ill-health but handed the business over to his son and daughter, Garrett and Margo Ann. 'He may not be here in body, but he's certainly here in spirit!' says Margo Ann. 'People ask about him and my mum every day.'

But the fruit and vegetable stall was only 'the day job' for Michael in the 1960s. By night he was an impresario, touring some of the biggest names of the 1960s and 1970s in Ireland, including Bridie Gallagher, a trailblazer on the Irish country music scene, and Ann Shelton, one of the greatest singers of 1940s and 1950s Britain. He is also credited with discovering Rory Gallagher, Ireland's legendary guitar genius. When Rory was only 14 years old he entered a talent competition, which was held in Cork City Hall. There were three judges on that night – Michael F. Murphy and two others. There was disagreement between two of the judges. Should a talented local opera singer win first prize, or should a long-haired 14-year-old electric guitarist win? Michael had the deciding vote – he chose the long-haired 14-year-old guitarist, and the rest, as they say, is history.

The stall now sells fresh fruit and vegetables, eggs, artisan products including homemade jams, lemonades, organic Irish rapeseed oil, organic Kilbeggan porridge, Irish handmade chocolates and sweets, gluten-free products from The Foods of Athenry, Gurmans Teas and Coffees, homemade bread and cakes and West Cork honey.

Baked Figs with Sticky Orange Glaze

A healthy and deliciously different dessert.

Serves 4

4–8 large figs
2 large oranges, for juice and zest
8 tbsp very low-fat plain fromage frais

Preheat the oven to 190°C/375°F/gas mark 5. Using a sharp knife, cut across the top of each fig, push the sides out lightly to open it up like a flower. Place into a large ovenproof dish. Finally, grate the zest from the oranges and sprinkle all but 1 tsp over the figs. Squeeze the juice over the figs.

Place into the oven to cook for 15–20 minutes, basting frequently with the orange juice until sticky and golden. Serve figs with the syrup drizzled over and a spoonful of fromage frais sprinkled with the reserved zest.

Easy Mango and Passion Fruit Mousse

Serves 6

2 large ripe mangos
4 passion fruit, halved
3 large egg whites
300g/11oz Greek yoghurt

Remove the mango flesh from the large central stone and peel. Place half of the mango into a food processor and blitz until smooth. Stir the flesh of one of the passion fruit, seeds and all, into the purée.

Using a sharp knife, dice the remaining mango into small cubes.

In a clean bowl whisk the egg whites until stiff. Gently fold in the yoghurt, mango cubes and half of the purée with a metal spoon.

Fill six dishes or glasses with alternate layers of mousse and mango purée. Top each one with the pulp from half a passion fruit. Serve immediately or chill for up to 6 hours. If chilling, add passion fruit topping just before serving.

Battle of the Brown Breads

There must be as many Irish brown bread recipes in existence as there are seashells on the seashore. Every cook or chef professes to have the best recipe in existence. Here are three brown bread recipes, all of which have been tested at least three times and all of which are very good. If you think you have a better recipe than any of these, then I'd love to hear from you!

Guinness Brown Bread

A robust savoury-tasting bread, great served with cheese or as an accompaniment to soup.

60g/2oz plain white flour
350g/12oz wholemeal flour
30g/2oz pinhead oatmeal
30g/2oz wheat bran
1 tsp salt
2 tbsp brown sugar
1 tsp baking soda
1 tbsp treacle
30g/2oz butter
300ml/½ pint Guinness
100ml/3½fl oz buttermilk, or full-fat milk

Preheat the oven to 190°C/375°F/gas mark 5. Grease and line a 2lb loaf tin.
Put the flours, oatmeal, bran, salt and sugar in a mixing bowl and stir. Sift in the soda and mix with a wooden spoon.

Melt the treacle and butter together in a saucepan over a low heat, then take off the heat and add the Guinness. Stir well.

Now add the milk and the Guinness and treacle to the dry ingredients and stir well. Transfer the mixture to the loaf tin and bake for about 40–50 minutes. Test with a skewer to see if cooked. If the skewer comes out clean after inserting into the middle of the bread, then the bread is cooked. If the skewer comes out with some dough on it, it needs more time in the oven.

Wrap in a clean tea towel and allow to cool.

Irish Brown Soda Bread

The traditional Irish brown bread. Spread a slice liberally with butter and homemade jam or marmalade.

225g/8oz wholemeal flour
225g/8oz plain white flour
1 tsp baking soda
1 tsp salt
375/400ml/a little over ½ pint buttermilk

Preheat the oven to 230°C/445°F/gas mark 8.

Put the wholemeal flour into a large mixing bowl and sieve in the white flour, then the salt, sugar and soda. Mix together well.

Make a well in the middle of the flour and pour in about three-quarters of the buttermilk. With your fingers, draw the flour into the milk, mixing as lightly as possible. The dough should come together easily into a soft ball. If you find that it is a little too dry, then add a little milk and work it in again. Be careful not to add too much milk, though, otherwise the mixture will become too sticky.

Turn the dough onto a floured board and work it into an oval shape with your hands. It should be about 2 inches (7cm) in height. Cut a large cross in the surface, and place in the centre of the oven on a lightly floured baking tray.

After about 10 minutes, reduce the heat to 200°C/390°F/gas mark 6. Bake for another 30 minutes. Remove from the oven and hold it upside down in a clean tea towel. Knock on the base of the loaf – if it sounds hollow, it is done. If not, return to the oven for 5–10 minutes more.

Wrap in a clean tea towel and allow to cool.

Healthy Brown Bread Loaf

A good general all-rounder that goes with soups and preserves alike.

450g/1lb plain flour
1 level tsp of salt
300g/11oz course wholemeal flour
50g/2oz wheat bran
40g/1½oz wheat germ
40g/1½oz porridge oats
40g/1½oz brown sugar
1 tbsp bread soda
2 level tsp baking powder
500ml/18fl oz buttermilk
sesame seeds to sprinkle on top of the loaf

Preheat the oven to 180°C/355°F/gas mark 4 and grease or line a 2lb loaf tin with baking parchment.

Sieve the plain flour and salt into a large bowl. Add the wholemeal flour, wheat bran and germ, oats, soda and baking powder and mix well. Make a well in the centre of the flour and pour in the buttermilk, mixing lightly with your hands.

Spoon the mixture into the loaf tin and sprinkle the top with sesame seeds.

Bake in the centre of the oven for 1 hour. Test with a skewer and, if it comes out with no trace of mixture on it, then the loaf is cooked. If there is a little dough on the skewer, give the loaf another 10–15 minutes.

Wrap in a clean tea towel and allow to cool.

K. O'Connell Ltd

Stalls 52–56

This very attractive and award-winning fish stall has grown steadily both in size and reputation since its inception in the early 1960s. Today, it ranks as probably the most famous fish stall in both Ireland and the UK, as even Queen Elizabeth was drawn to admire its vast array of fish on her visit to the English Market on 20 May 2011.

Indisputably, another great attraction that the stall has to offer is the exuberant and ever-smiling Mr Pat O'Connell, whose charm and quick wit could be described as 'even sharper than his filleting knife'. Pat always has a quip or a wink for even the most serious of shoppers, ensuring that not only do they leave his stall with the freshest of fish, but also displaying a rather large and satisfied smile.

On any given day the stall carries at least forty different varieties of fish, many caught in the waters off Castletownbere and Union Hall in West Cork. Many top celebrity

chefs will refuse to leave Cork without paying a visit to this iconic Cork fish stall. Darina and Rachel Allen, Clodagh McKenna, Rick Stein and Martin Shanahan are all devotees, to mention but a few.

The stall was first founded in 1962 by a young Cork mother who had a strong desire to 'be her own boss'. Her name was Kathleen (or Kay) O'Connell. Kay, who could never have been described as work-shy, was the daughter of hard-working Cork business people. She was eager to make her own mark on the city and, with the help of her husband, the newly-married couple did just that when they opened a fish stall in the English Market.

Today Kathleen's sons, Pat and Paul, carry on the family tradition of knowledgeable staff, strong work ethic and a passion for fresh fish. Trade at the stall is always brisk and the banter with customers is always lively.

The brothers continue to build on the success of their mother with constant innovation and product variation. Today Paul's son Seán and Pat's daughter Emma help to run the stall under the watchful eye of their parents to ensure that Kay O'Connell's legacy is kept alive and kicking in the English Market.

Recently, the stall has opened a new gourmet speciality counter selling freshly made paella, squid salad, crab salad, caviar, blinis, homemade fish stock, as well as oven-ready meals. Fish cakes and fish pies are freshly made at O'Connell's stall in the Market each morning.

O'Connell's Lemon Sole Fillets with Dublin Bay Prawns

A real treat from the sea. Light and delicious, this melt-in-the mouth seafood recipe is definitely one to try.

Serves 4

8 skinned fillets of lemon sole
salt and black pepper
16 shelled Dublin Bay prawns
300ml/½ pint fish stock
250ml/9fl oz white wine
100ml/3½ fl oz cream
50g/2oz butter, cut into cubes
lime or lemon, fresh dill or fennel to garnish

Preheat the oven to 180°C/355°F/gas mark 4. Place the sole fillets on a lightly oiled oven tray and season with salt and pepper. Place two shelled prawns in the middle of each fillet and roll the fillet so that the two prawns are surrounded with the sole. You can hold each rolled fillet in place with a toothpick if you feel the fillets need to be secured. Add about half the wine to the oven tray, cover with tin foil and place in the centre of the oven for 8–10 minutes.

For the sauce

Pour the fish stock into a pot and simmer until reduced. Add the remaining wine and reduce for another 5–8 minutes. Next add the cream and butter, one at a time, stirring until everything is fully incorporated. Taste and season.

Place two fillets of sole on each plate and drizzle with the sauce. Garnish with lemon or lime and dill.

Serve with steamed baby potatoes and roasted asparagus. A chilled Chardonnay or Riesling would complement this dish nicely.

O'Connell's Delicious Fish Pie

This is a five-star recipe for fish pie. Be warned, though, once you've tried this, no other fish pie will do. If you haven't time to make this from scratch, O'Connell's make fresh takeaway portions every morning at their gourmet counter.

Serves 4–6

5–6 medium to large potatoes, cooked and mashed with butter and milk
 and seasoned with salt and pepper
1 medium onion, diced
20ml rapeseed oil
500ml/18 floz fish stock
1 leek, chopped finely
2 sticks of celery, chopped finely
2 carrots, chopped finely
½ fennel bulb, chopped finely
1 lemon, juice and zest
75g/3oz cornflour
a little oil for frying
1kg mixed fish

Boil the potatoes and mash with milk and butter, season well with salt and pepper.
Preheat the oven to 180°C/355°F/gas mark 4.

Fry the onions gently in a little oil, add the fish stock, leek, celery, fennel, carrots and the lemon juice and zest. Allow everything to simmer for 10–15 minutes. Finally, take a little of the cooking liquid from the pot and add to the cornflour to make a paste. Add to the sauce, stirring all the while. Lastly add the mixed fish and allow to cook for 5 minutes. Pour the fish and sauce into an oven-to-table casserole dish and cover with the mashed potato. Bake in the centre of the oven for 20 minutes.

Red Mullet with Sautéed Pak Choi

Found in the Mediterranean Sea and also in the East North Atlantic – generally between Wexford and Cork – the red mullet, despite its name, is not even remotely related to the common grey mullet. Unusually for a fish, the liver of the red mullet is considered a delicacy in its own right, especially in Mediterranean countries. Red mullet is good grilled, shallow-fried or oven-baked.

Serves 2

1–2 red mullet
1 pak choi
1 garlic clove, crushed
2 tbsp soy sauce
1 tsp fish sauce
1–2 finely chopped spring onions to garnish
lemon or lime for serving

Heat a little oil in a frying pan, place the fish in the pan and fry on both sides for about 3 minutes each.

Chop the pak choi and fry in a wok or hot frying pan, then add the garlic, soy and fish sauces. Toss for about 1 minute and then serve immediately. Place a little of the pak choi stir-fry on each plate and lay the fish on top. Sprinkle with chopped spring onion and serve with lemon or lime.

Stephen Landon

Stall P8

Stephen Landon has been trading in the English Market for twenty years, supplying only top-quality pork products. Pork has always been a popular dish with Cork cooks, and in recent times immigrants to the city have ensured that it is as popular today as it was in former times. Stephen sells loin of pork, pork ribs, bacon rib, as well as hams at Christmas time.

'In all my years trading in the Market, I have seen businesses come and businesses go and in my opinion the only businesses that have not succeeded in the English Market are those who are not selling top-quality products. If the quality is there, the business will survive,' says Stephen.

Stephen Landon's Simply Delicious Smoked Bacon

Moist, succulent smoked bacon with a sweet and sticky honey glaze.

Serves 4

1 joint of Stephen Landon's smoked bacon – enough for 4 people
8 carrots, roughly chopped
2 small or 1 medium turnip, roughly chopped
3 tbsp Irish honey
2 tbsp brown sugar

Place the bacon joint in a large saucepan of cold water – the larger your saucepan, the better. Turn the heat to high and let the saucepan come to the boil, then turn down the heat, cover the saucepan and allow the joint to cook at a gentle bubble. Cook like this for 1 hour.

After 1 hour of cooking, place a steamer or colander over the saucepan and fill it with the turnip and carrots. Cover the steamer/colander with the saucepan lid and allow to cook for 20–30 minutes more. The vegetables will take on a subtle flavour of the smoked bacon.

Put the cooked vegetables in a serving dish and keep warm. Lift the bacon from the water and place on a roasting dish. Mix the brown sugar with the honey, and cover the top of the bacon with half of the honey and sugar paste. Place in a hot oven (220°C/430°F/gas mark 6) for 5 minutes. Remove the bacon from the oven, cover it with the remainder of the honey and sugar mix and place back into the oven for another 5–10 minutes. Allow to rest for 10–15 minutes, covered with foil, before carving. Serve with the steamed vegetables.

Bacon and Mushroom Pasta with a 'Secret' Market Sauce

Stephen can't recall where exactly he got this recipe from but, whenever he serves it, compliments come rolling in. It is worth trying this recipe, as it really is very, very good indeed!

Serves 4

1 large saucepan boiling water
500g/1lb pasta
200g/7oz mushrooms, sliced
150g/5oz bacon lardons or back rashers, cubed
1 carton (200ml/7fl oz) crème fraîche, or single cream
50ml/2fl oz milk
20ml or 2 tablespoons soy sauce (Stephen recommends Kikkoman Soy Sauce, available at Mr Bell's)
a few grinds of black pepper
no salt required (the soy sauce and bacon bring enough salt to this dish)
chopped parsley to garnish
Parmesan shavings to garnish

First, wash and chop the parsley and make the Parmesan shavings by running a vegetable peeler along the corner of a wedge of Parmesan. Prepare enough to garnish 4 dishes.

Add the penne pasta to a large saucepan of boiling water, stirring occasionally so that the pasta does not stick together. While the pasta is cooking, wipe the mushrooms with kitchen paper.

Heat a large frying pan with no oil and add the bacon lardons/rashers and cook, stirring frequently. When the bacon is cooked, after about 2 minutes, add the sliced mushrooms and continue to cook for 2 minutes more, then add the crème fraîche/cream, the milk and the soy sauce and turn the heat down to low.

When the pasta is cooked, strain it in a colander and divide between 4 large plates or pasta bowls. Pour the bacon and mushroom sauce over the pasta and finish by garnishing with the chopped parsley and Parmesan shavings and some ground black pepper if you wish.

Serve with garlic bread.

Bacon and Cabbage Soup with Mustard

A very tasty starter if you are planning to serve a light main course.
A soup with both 'eating and drinking' in it.

Serves 4

1 medium onion, finely diced
50g/2oz butter
3 large potatoes, peeled and diced
250g savoy or spring cabbage (about 1 small cabbage)
1 litre/1¾ pints chicken or ham stock
2 bay leaves
175g/6oz cooked ham or bacon, cut into chunky pieces
1 tsp English mustard, optional
salt and black pepper to season

Sweat the onion in the butter for 3–4 minutes. Add the potato and cabbage. Cook, stirring constantly, for another 2–3 minutes. Add the stock and bay leaves.

Bring to the boil and then reduce to a simmer until the potatoes are soft. Remove the bay leaves and liquidise the soup – a hand blender will do or you can push it through a sieve if you don't have a blender.

Add the cooked ham or bacon and stir into the soup with a teaspoon of mustard. Leave to simmer for 5 minutes. Season with salt and black pepper. Serve with fresh crusty bread.

O'Flynn's
Gourmet Sausage
Company

Stall 23

O'Flynn's Gourmet Sausage stall is found at the very centre of the Market. You can't miss it, because you will smell the delicious savoury aromas wafting from the stall even before you see it. Let your nose be your guide!

Declan O'Flynn heads up this family business together with his wife Anne and his brothers, David and Steven. Declan is proud to say that he was born with a genetic predisposition to become a sausage maker. His grandfather William O'Flynn trained with one of Ireland's most famous sausage-makers, Henry Denny, and was responsible for earning the Denny company its first gold medal for sausages in the 1920s. Declan's father then followed in the family footsteps and ran a small business preparing tripe and drisheen and making sausages in his kitchen in the Shandon area of Cork. He supplied all the local butchers with his products.

In 1994 Declan, who had trained as a chef, decided it was time to 'grasp the sausage' and see if he could succeed in business. He rummaged through kitchen drawers and boxes in the attic of the family home and managed to find most of his father's prized sausage recipes. With the help of other family members, the O'Flynns managed to build up a formidable sausage business, which has garnered a host of awards from the Association of Craft Butcher's of Ireland. In 2003 the family opened a stall in the English Market selling freshly cooked sausages with sauces and fried onions. In 2010 they opened another shop, not far from the market, on Winthrop Street.

All meat for O'Flynn's handmade sausages is sourced in Cork and Waterford and spices are supplied by Mr Bell's stall in the English Market. Declan has had fun creating his own recipes and these include:

The Cork Boi – a sausage in celebration of Cork city, made with best pork and beef and flavoured with Murphy's stout.

The Blackwater – a sausage made with pork, black pudding and apple developed in conjunction with chef Paul Flynn of the Tannery Cookery School and Restaurant in Dungarvan.

The Traditional Irish – great local pork delicately seasoned with mild spices.

The Sweet Italian – pork with paprika, garlic, fennel and herbs (95 per cent meat).

The Lamb Merguez – a North African-style sausage with hints of mint, coriander, lemon and chilli.

The Habanero and Green Chilli Sausage – A spicy sausage with a Mexican kick.

'Being proud sausage makers from the "People's Republic of Cork", we were thrilled to be awarded the Great Taste Winner for our Cork Boi sausage,' says Declan. 'It encapsulates the best of us, our family and Cork city, as it came from an old family recipe using Irish pork, beef and Cork's famous Murphy's stout, locally grown herbs and seasonings.'

O'Flynn's Gourmet Sausages with Hot Potatoes and Aioli

A great lunchtime favourite with many Corkonians, this dish is also available at O'Flynn's Gourmet Sausage Grill on Winthrop Street.

Serves 4

8 O'Flynn's gourmet sausages
4 tbsp olive oil
1 kg baby potatoes
1 green pepper, sliced
1 red pepper, sliced
1 onion, sliced
2 level tbsp paprika
salt and cracked black pepper

For the aioli

5 tbsp mayonnaise
1 clove of garlic (crushed)
1 tsp paprika

Put your sausages without oil on the tray in a preheated oven at 200°C/390°F/gas mark 6 for about 20 minutes.

Meanwhile bring your baby potatoes to the boil and allow to simmer. Make sure not to over-cook them – they should be a little under done. Strain and leave under running water to cool. When cool enough to handle, halve the potatoes.

In a hot pan add the oil, potatoes, green and red pepper, onion, paprika and salt and pepper and stir until cooked through. You can cook them longer if you would like them to be a little more crispy. To make the aoili, mix the mayonnaise, garlic and paprika together in a bowl.
Serve 2 sausages each, with the hot potatoes and aioli on the side.

For this recipe we would recommend any of our spicy sausages: Sweet Italian, Mexican Chorizo, Cajun Andouille or Spicy Mediterranean or just mix and match. None of our 95 per cent meat sausages contain wheat, so this recipe can be used for anyone with a wheat intolerance. Ask any of the staff at our stall and they will help you with this.

O'Flynn's Bangers and Mash

An Irish comfort food classic and always a big hit with all the family. The gourmet sausages transform an everyday staple into a gourmet feast. This dish is prepared fresh every day at O'Flynn's stall in the English Market and also at their grill on Winthrop Street.

Serves 4

8 O'Flynn's gourmet sausages (choose from over 30 varieties)
We recommend:
Cork Boi: pork and beef sausage with Cork's famous Murphy's stout, onions & thyme
The Cumberland: pork with sage and black pepper
Pork and Leek: pork with fresh leeks
All our sausages are made using 75–95 per cent of local meats only.

For the mash:
800g/2lb rooster potatoes, peeled and quartered
salt and white pepper

Quick and simple onion gravy:
500ml/18fl oz water
4 tbsp gravy granules
1 onion, sliced
add 100ml/3½ fl oz red wine if you wish to give it a kick
black pepper

Put your sausages in a preheated oven at 200°C/390°F/gas mark 6 for about 20 minutes.
For the mash, bring your potatoes to the boil and let them slowly simmer for 20 minutes. Strain, then add the butter and mash together. Season with salt and pepper and give the mash a quick stir with a wooden spoon.

For the gravy, bring the water to the boil, turn down to a simmer and whisk in the gravy granules for about 1 minute.

Add your sliced onions, and red wine if you wish, and simmer for 10 minutes.

Serve the mash with the sausages and onion gravy. This is also very good served with peas.
As Declan says 'Pure Cork comfort food, boy!'

About Garlic

Garlic or *Allium sativum* has been cultivated since ancient times. In ancient Egypt it is said that Egyptian masters fed garlic to their slaves to increase the workers' physical power. Today it is used as a popular flavouring in cooking and may be eaten raw or cooked.

There are many different varieties of garlic available. The most common (and the one with the strongest flavour) is the white-skinned garlic. The slightly less pungent purple-skinned garlic is mainly grown in Italy and Mexico.

Garlic's medicinal uses are many, including as a digestive stimulant, diuretic and antispasmodic. Additionally, many studies have been done that show the value of garlic in preventing certain forms of cancer as well as being beneficial to heart health. A BBC documentary in 2007 outlined the reputed benefits of garlic to general health and well-being, and indicated that garlic may have other beneficial properties, such as preventing and fighting the common cold. This is a long-held belief in the fields of homeopathic and herbal medicine.

In cooking, few other ingredients seem to offer as complex a range of flavours as garlic. Cooks can vary the amount of garlic flavour released by the way they prepare and use it. The more juices and oils extracted from the garlic, the more garlic flavour will be incorporated into the food.

Pressing

Garlic put through a garlic press or puréed releases the most garlic oils and therefore provides the strongest garlic flavour. Suitable for robust casseroles, curries and soups.

Crushing

A pestle and mortar is ideal for crushing garlic. This method releases the pungent flavour and natural juices of garlic. Good for use in sauces when you want a strong garlic flavour, similar to pressing.

Minced

Finely minced garlic will release more oils than chopped or sliced garlic, but less than pressed or crushed. Great for flavouring oil to be used for sautéing.

Chopped

The chopping process does not extract a large amount of juice or oil. The amount of flavour obtained will depend on how small the garlic is chopped and therefore allowed to dissolve in the cooking process. This method is good for use in salsas and stir-frys when you don't want the garlic flavour to dominate the dish.

Slicing

Slices or larger pieces of garlic won't completely dissolve when cooked, resulting in a lighter garlic flavour. Best used in fish dishes or salads when you require a milder garlic flavour, but make sure to slice the garlic very thinly.

Browning

Garlic browned in oil imparts a very strong nutty flavour. While some recipes suggest browning, others will warn against it. Try browning some minced garlic in a small amount of olive oil and see if you like the flavour.

If you are a garlic enthusiast, then you may be interested to know that the dishes which tend to have the most 'garlicy' flavour are: garlic potatoes, garlic mushrooms, garlic bread, garlic prawns and garlic butter.

Bon Appétit!

Tim O'Sullivan

Stalls 7 & 8

Tim O'Sullivan's grandfather Paddy first opened for business as a butcher in Cork in 1943. When he was old enough to join the family business, Tim's father served his apprenticeship under his father, and eventually took over the family business when Paddy retired. In the late 1980s Tim Jr served his apprenticeship under the watchful eye of his father. He is now the third-generation butcher in the O'Sullivan family. Tim's beef, lamb, pork and bacon are locally sourced and Tim prepares stir-fries, kebabs, meatloaf and beef roulade at his stall each morning for customers who require wholesome, easy-cook meals in a hurry.

Apricot-Stuffed Belly of Pork with Sautéed Savoy Cabbage ⟲

If you like crispy crackling, then you certainly will enjoy this recipe. If, however, you prefer your meat to be on the leaner side, then you could substitute the pork belly in this recipe for loin of pork.

Serves 6

50ml/2fl oz water
1.6kg (3½lb) pork belly or pork loin, boned, rolled and the skin scored (your butcher will do this)
1 small onion, chopped
1 clove of garlic
oil for frying
1 handful of parsley, chopped
75g/3oz (or about 8) dried apricots
75g/3oz breadcrumbs
sea salt and freshly ground black pepper to season
2 tsp fennel seeds
125ml/4fl oz apple juice
some butcher's string for tying up the joint

For the sauce
6 additional dried apricots
1 large Bramley cooking apple
124ml/4fl oz chicken stock
25g/1oz butter
5ml/1 tsp oil
1 head of Savoy cabbage, washed and finely sliced

Heat the oven to 200°C/425°F/gas mark 7. Pour a little boiling water over the skin of the pork, then pat dry with kitchen towel. This will help the crackling to become extra crispy.

Fry off the chopped onion and garlic in a saucepan with a drizzle of oil until softened.

Chop the parsley and the apricots (not too finely) and add to the saucepan with the onion and garlic. Next, add the breadcrumbs and stir well to combine all the ingredients. Season well with salt and pepper. Fill the centre of the pork with the stuffing and then roll it up like a swiss roll. Tie the joint at various intervals with string so that it will 'knit' together when cooking.

Place the joint in a roasting dish and season the top, the fatty side, with salt, pepper and a sprinkling of fennel seeds. Pour the apple juice into the roasting dish and sprinkle in 5–6 whole dried apricots. Slice a cooking apple into quarters and add to the roasting dish (no need to peel and core).

Roast in the preheated oven at 200°C/400°F/gas mark 6 for about 25 minutes and then reduce the heat to 180°C/350°F/gas mark 4 and roast for a further hour. When the pork is cooked, remove it from the roasting dish and place on a warm serving platter. Cover with tin foil and allow it to rest for 10 minutes.

To make the sauce, pour the fat and juices from the roasting dish into a jug and sit it in a basin of cold water so that the fat rises to the top. After about 2–3 minutes, you should be able to see the fat on the top half of the liquid; you can now spoon this off into a bowl and use at a later date for roasting potatoes or potato wedges.

Next, pass all the remaining liquid through a sieve back into the roasting dish. Push the pulp of the apple and apricots through the sieve also. Add the chicken stock and bring to the boil, then reduce the heat and allow the liquid to reduce on a low simmer for about 3–4 minutes. Season to taste and serve with the pork.

For the sautéed cabbage, in a wok or a large deep saucepan melt the butter and add in the oil. Tip in the washed and sliced cabbage and toss frequently until the cabbage wilts and reduces slightly (this might take 4–6 minutes), then serve immediately with the pork.

Búachaill Dána Burger

Tim guarantees that, once you've tried this burger, there is simply no going back.
A real crowd-pleaser and a great quick family meal.

Makes 6 medium burgers or 4 extra large

enough oil for frying
1 onion, finely chopped
2 cloves garlic, crushed
450g/1lb minced beef
2 tbsp tomato ketchup
salt and pepper
1 egg, beaten
burger buns
lettuce, chopped
2 tomatoes, sliced
slices of cheddar, optional

Heat the oil in a saucepan over a moderate heat. Add the chopped onion and crushed garlic. Cook the onions for 4–5 minutes until soft. Remove the onions and garlic from the pan and set aside to cool.

When cool, add to the mincemeat with the tomato ketchup, salt and pepper and beaten egg. Mix well and then mould the mix into burgers with your hands.

Over a high heat, add some rapeseed oil to a heavy-based frying pan and fry the burgers on both sides until they are well browned.

Place in a preheated oven, 180°C/355°F/gas mark 4, and leave for 10–15 minutes until cooked through. The cooking time depends on the thickness of the burgers, but the juices should run clear when the burgers are pierced with a fork.

Serve in a lightly toasted burger bun with a squeeze of ketchup, a little lettuce and freshly sliced tomato and a slice of cheese.

Superfruit

Stalls 17, 18 & 19

uperfruit is a large fruit, vegetable and flower stall just inside the Grand Parade entrance to the English Market. The very affable Mr Michael Corrigan is the owner. Michael opened his stall on 1 December 1969 and has been enjoying brisk trade ever since. For the past few years, Michael has seen the Market change from a place that sold mainly meat and vegetables to one that now provides everything from fine wines to spices and Mediterranean olives. When Michael began trading, he says that most Irish people did not know what a red pepper was or what to do with it. Now Michael stocks exotic fruits and vegetables from all over the world and people just can't seem to get enough of them.

But Michael is not only known for the exotic. His ability to sniff out the first crop of British Queens of the season leaves hoteliers and restaurateurs scratching their heads in disbelief.

Orange and Mint Salad

A very different yet surprisingly refreshing salad with a hint of the Middle East. An excellent side dish with mackerel or salmon.

Serves 4

6 blood oranges, peeled, pith removed
2–3 tsp orange-blossom water (available at Mr Bell's)
2 tbsp orange peel, cut into thin matchsticks
3 tbsp caster sugar
150ml/15fl oz water
leaves from a bunch of fresh mint, finely shredded
100g/4oz blanched almonds, sliced, to decorate

Slice the peeled oranges thinly, removing any pips. Arrange on a serving platter or dish and sprinkle with the orange-blossom water.

In a small saucepan, mix together the orange peel, sugar, water and mint and simmer over a low heat for 15 minutes.

When the sauce has cooled, pour it over the oranges and decorate with the almonds.

Exotic Fruit Pavlova

Everybody loves Pavlova, but why not give it a bit of a make-over by using some luscious exotic fruits? A refreshingly light and delicious dessert.

Serves 4–6

1 passion fruit
1 kiwi fruit
½ orange
½ star fruit
300ml/½ pint of cream
350g/12oz caster sugar
finely grated rind of ½ orange
4 large strawberries
sprigs of mint to decorate

For the meringue

3 large egg whites, at room temperature
a pinch of salt
350g/12oz caster sugar
1 tsp cornflour
1 tsp white wine vinegar
2 drops vanilla extract

Preheat the oven to 150°C/300°F/gas mark 2. Line a baking sheet with non-stick baking parchment and draw a 9-inch/22cm circle (use a plate as a guide).

To make the meringue, whisk the egg whites and salt in a large clean bowl until stiff peaks have formed. Whisk in the sugar, a quarter at a time, whisking well after each addition, until stiff and very shiny.

Sprinkle in the cornflour, vinegar and vanilla extract and gently fold in with a metal spoon. Pile the meringue on to the paper within the circle, making sure there is a substantial hollow in the centre.

Place in the oven and immediately reduce the heat to 120°C/250°F/gas mark ½ and continue to cook for 1½–2 hours until crisp but a little soft in the centre. Turn off the oven and leave to cool completely.

To make the filling, halve the passion fruit and scoop out the pulp into a small bowl. Peel and slice the kiwi fruit, segment the orange and cut the star fruit into slices.

Place the cream in a bowl with the sugar and orange rind and whip until thickened. To serve, peel the paper off the Pavlova and transfer to a serving plate. Pile on the cream and arrange all of the prepared fruit and berries on top, finishing with the passion fruit pulp and slices of strawberry. Decorate with the mint sprigs, then cut into slices and arrange on serving plates.

The Chicken Inn

Stalls 12, 13 & 24

Tim Mulcahy runs The Chicken Inn side by side with his father Jack and his mother Mary. One of the largest stalls in the English Market, the family sell whole chickens, chicken breasts, legs, wings and anything you care to mention that is chicken-related. They also sell eggs, ham hock, duck, turkey and a little pork, as well as Tim's award-winning ham. A very popular choice with customers is Tim's fillet of chicken stuffed with black pudding and wrapped in bacon. The Chicken Inn was established in the mid-1950s by Tim's grandfather (Mary's father), John Lane, who began by selling poultry, eggs and butter. He sourced his supplies at country markets in Millstreet and Macroom and also directly from farms on the outskirts of the city.

Mary Mulcahy began working in the Market on leaving school and continues to work there today, some 57 years later. In days gone by, Mary says there was good trade in older hens who were past laying and these were used as boiling fowl and for making chicken broth, which was seen as a great tonic for the sick and elderly. Today there is more of a diverse customer base in the market, with many students and workers from abroad preferring to shop in the English Market instead of shopping in supermarkets. Students from abroad say that they enjoy the chat and banter in the Market and it helps them to improve their English.

Tim says that the recent worldwide surge of interest in food and cooking is very noticeable at his stall. In a recent Jamie Oliver cookery programme, Jamie recommended 'Supreme of Chicken' for a particular dish. According to Tim, sales for 'Supreme of Chicken' went through the roof for a couple of weeks after that programme aired. Duck is also a very popular choice in recent times with many people preferring to entertain at home rather than eating out.

Roast Turkey with Thyme and Onion Stuffing

Turkey is the traditional bird for Christmas and large family gatherings. Tim shares his step-by-step guide for cooking the perfect turkey.

Serves 12–14

7kg turkey, oven-ready
salt, black pepper and a little flour
2 tbsp softened butter
6 slices streaky bacon

For the stuffing
450g/2lb bread broken into pieces
5 tbsp fresh chopped parsley
2 tbsp fresh chopped thyme
1 medium onion, quartered
salt and black pepper
150g/5oz melted butter

For the gravy
giblets, retained from the turkey
1 small onion, peeled and quartered
1 bay leaf
salt and pepper
1 tbsp flour
1 tbsp wine

To make the stuffing

Put the bread, parsley, thyme and onion in a food processor. Blitz all the ingredients until the onion is finely chopped and the bread has become breadcrumbs. Season the stuffing mixture and stir in the melted butter.

To stuff the turkey

Preheat the oven to 220°C/430°F/gas mark 7.

Place the turkey in a large oiled roasting tin, remove the giblets and livers – check both ends of the bird for these. Loosen the skin at the neck with your hands. Pack the stuffing into the bird. When the cavity is full, tuck the remaining skin underneath the bird. Any remaining stuffing can be cooked in an oven-proof dish covered with foil in the oven 30 minutes before the turkey is due to have finished cooking.

To cook the turkey

Pour a generous drizzle of good-quality oil (Irish rapeseed or olive) all over the turkey. Season well with salt and pepper and then lay the rashers of bacon over the breasts. Cover the turkey in tin foil and place in the oven to roast. Allow 30–40 minutes per kilo. After 30 minutes, reduce the temperature

of the oven to 180°C/355°F/gas mark 3. For the last half-hour of cooking, remove the turkey from the oven, baste and then place back in the oven without the foil.

To check if the turkey is cooked, make an incision (with a sharp knife) where the leg is connected to the body of the bird – the juices should run clear. If you think the bird could do with a little more time in the oven, put it back in but remember to cover it once again with the foil, or the skin may burn.

When you are satisfied that the turkey is cooked, remove it from the oven and transfer it to a serving platter. Cover it with foil and allow it to rest whilst you make the gravy.

To make the gravy

Use the giblets from the turkey to make a good stock. Place the giblets, a small onion and a bay leaf in a saucepan. Cover the giblets with cold water and simmer gently for 1½ hours. Strain and season. You can prepare this stock the day before or even a couple of days before you require it and have it in your fridge ready to use.

Having removed the turkey from the roasting tin, spoon off the fat with a large spoon or ladle until only the juices remain. Over a medium heat, stir in a tablespoon of flour and a tablespoon of wine. Stir vigorously until the mixture resembles a smooth paste, then add the stock and continue to cook for 2–3 minutes. Taste and season with salt and pepper.

Delicious Succulent Honey-Glazed Ham

Another classic for any family gathering. The cider and apple juice make for a wonderfully succulent and unforgettable ham. Reduce the ingredients as necessary if you opt for a smaller size ham and always poach in enough liquid to cover the ham.

Serves 12

enough water to cover the ham after the cider and apple juice have been added
7kg unsmoked ham
1½ litres/2¼ pints apple juice
1½ litres/2¼ pints cider
1 tbsp cloves
4 cooking apples, halved

For the glaze
225g/8oz brown sugar
225g/8 tbsp honey
1 tbsp English mustard
cloves to decorate

Pour about ½ litre/1 pint of water into a very large saucepan and then place the ham into the pot. The pot has to be large enough to accommodate the ham, with plenty of room to cover it with liquid. Add the apple juice, cider, cloves and apples and enough additional water to just cover the ham. Bring the ham to the boil, then reduce the heat and leave to simmer for 7 hours, or about 1 hour per kilo. Allow the ham to cool in the liquid and then tip out the liquid, which will make retrieving your ham a little easier.

Place the ham on a baking tray or roasting dish. Trim off some of the excess fat with a sharp knife, but leave a thin covering of fat all over. Preheat the oven to 200°C/390°F/gas mark 5. Put the sugar, honey and mustard into a small saucepan and bring to the boil. Allow to reduce by about a quarter. When the glaze has reduced it is ready to use.

Score the top of the ham with a knife, making diamond shapes. At the top and bottom points of each diamond, stick a clove into the ham. Brush or carefully pour some of the glaze over the ham and place in the oven for 10 minutes. Take the ham out, glaze again and place back in the oven for another 10 minutes. Now your ham is ready to serve.

Roast Goose with Apples and Prune Compote

A great alternative for Christmas dinner or for any special occasion. Goose is more moist and succulent than turkey and has a stronger flavour. Tim reckons that this goose recipe is fit for a king and is well worth trying. A 7kg goose generally takes 3 hours to cook.

Serves 8

1 large 6–7kg/14lb goose
1 large onion, chopped
2 celery sticks, chopped
1 tbsp black peppercorns
1 bay leaf or rosemary sprig, plus extra to garnish
4 medium cooking apples, cored
25g unsalted butter
50g firm-textured rustic bread
3 garlic cloves, crushed

2 tbsp chopped sage, plus extra
  to garnish
½ tsp ground cloves
1 lemon, finely grated zest
salt and black pepper
1 tbsp plain flour
250g/9oz pitted prunes
200ml/7fl oz port or marsala

Preheat the oven to 220°C/425°F/gas mark 7. Prick the underside of the bird with a skewer, especially around the parson's nose and the wings (this will help the excess fat to run off freely).

Put the goose on a large roasting rack over a large roasting tray and rub the skin with flour and plenty of seasoning. Cover the bird with a large piece of foil. Roast for 30 minutes. Then, reduce the temperature to 180°C/350°F/gas mark 4 and roast for a further 1½ hours. For the apples, melt the butter in a frying pan and fry the onion and celery until soft. Crumble the bread into the pan with the garlic, sage, cloves, lemon zest and seasoning and stir. Cut the top off the apples. Pack the mixture into and on top of the apples.

For the prune compote, put the prunes and port in a saucepan and slowly bring to the boil. Reduce the heat, leave to simmer for 5 minutes and then turn off the heat.

Remove the goose from the oven and pour off any excess fat into a container. Return the goose to the tin, put the apples around it and cook for a further hour. Test if the goose is cooked by pushing a skewer into the thickest part of the thigh – the juices should run clear. Transfer to a large platter, cover with foil and leave to stand for 20–30 minutes.

Serve with the apples and the prune compote.

A Short History of Dairying in Ireland

It is not without good reason that Ireland is known as 'the Emerald Isle'. Whilst grass cannot grow without water, this emerald isle of ours could never be accused of lacking in that department. However, it is not only the availability of year-round 'moisture' which is a contributory factor to Ireland having such lush pastures. The geographical location of the country also has a bearing on our rich soil and mild climate, which is influenced by the Gulf Stream, and also the all-important moisture-bearing south-westerly prevailing winds.

As far back in history as the third century, Ireland was famed for its green and fertile pastures, as Gaius Julius Solinus bore witness to his *De Mirabilibus Mundi* (The Wonders of the World). Solinus wrote: 'Ireland has such excellent pastures that cattle there are brought to the danger of their lives by overfeeding, except now and then they are driven out of the field.'

In Irish folklore, dairy products are also frequently referred to. An account of a cattle raid at Cooley describes how Queen Maeve of Connaught was 'mortally wounded by a skim milk cheese flung from the sling of her nephew'. Another story tells of an attempt on the life of Saint Patrick when he was offered a poisoned cheese! Interesting dairying times indeed...

Butter

Butter has always played an important part in the diet of the Irish – much more so than cheese. From 1770 to 1925 the Cork Butter Exchange played a significant role in the shaping of the city of Cork. Cork's harbour (the second largest natural harbour in the world, Sydney Harbour being the largest) attracted much wealth, trade and commerce and was the perfect port for welcoming large vessels carrying imports from mainland Europe, which upon unloading would depart fully stocked again with Irish exports. In 1741 a list of imports which

came through the port of Cork included: glass bottles, copper plates, ale and beer, almonds, cinnamon, cocoa nuts, nutmegs, raisins, lemons, oranges, tea, tobacco, wines from all over Europe, cotton and mohair.

Exports for that same year included: 73,108 barrels of beef, 50,917 containers of butter, 4,978 containers of candles, 26 tons of salmon, 138,788 yards of linen cloth, 10,360 barrels of pork, 1,563 dozen tongues and 592 stone of wool, to mention but a few.

At 6 o'clock each morning, the Butter Market would open its doors and farmers from all over southern Ireland would jostle for a place in the queue, ready to sell the butter which they had brought in wooden barrels, or 'firkins' as they were then called. Records from the seventeenth century show that vast amounts of butter was being exported from the port of Cork to mainland Europe and from there it was often re-shipped across the Atlantic. During the 1700s and 1800s, ships from Sweden, Denmark, Holland, France, Portugal and Spain frequently called at Cork harbour to take butter to their colonies. At that time, the Cork Butter Market was one of the most famous butter markets in the world.

Imagine then at this time large ships docking in Cork harbour, ready to load up with butter from the Cork Butter Exchange. Where better for them to stock up the ship's own supplies than at the English Market? Corned mutton, spiced beef, corned beef, tongues in brine and salted fish were all ready to be loaded on board these enormous vessels and would be well preserved for even the lengthiest of voyages.

Cheese

Cheesemaking in Ireland has had almost as tumultuous a history as the people of Ireland. It certainly closely mirrors the history of Ireland from the seventeenth century up until recent times.

The Romans may have brought the art of cheesemaking to Ireland, but they were appalled that the native Iverni (Irish) were not as enamoured with cheese as they themselves, and referred to the Irish as 'barbarous butter eaters'.

However, by medieval times it is well documented that cheesemaking was widespread in Ireland, with the monks in the many monasteries perfecting the art. But Ireland's budding love affair with cheese was about to come to an abrupt end. The plantations of the 1700s, in which Ireland was settled with English landlords and the local landowners were driven off their land, brought indigenous Irish cheesemaking to a sudden halt. It was not until 1889 that cheesemaking underwent a temporary revival, thanks to the co-operative movement founded by Sir Horace Plunkett. Cheddar and Caerphilly-style cheeses were produced en masse but were mostly intended for the export market to supply Britain with cheeses during First World War. However, post-war, and after the Irish War of Independence (1921), the market for Irish cheese in Britain had slumped severely. This was due to the fact that Britain and Ireland embarked on a five-year trade war with one another and the British returned to making and supplying their own cheeses. Large-scale Irish cheesemaking was again abandoned indefinitely.

Fast forward then to 1970s Ireland: floral-shirted men with long hair and ladies in maxi dresses roamed the Irish country roads in Volkswagen mini-vans looking for a little plot of land to call their own. Their mantra, it seems, was 'peace, love and . . . cheese'. They yearned to become self-sufficient and live off the land, far away from commerce and greed. Many of these new arrivals settled in West Cork and many of them were not Irish by birth. Thanks to these new renaissance cheesemakers, Ireland can now compete competently on the world cheese stage, offering delicious and interesting 'new' alternatives to the more established 'old' world cheeses. The founding fathers (and mothers!) of this new Irish cheesemaking revolution are: Veronica and Norman Steele – Milleens; Dick and Helene Willems – Coolea; Jeffa Gill – Durrus; Ed Harper – Cáis Chléire; Bill Hogan and Seán Ferry – Gabriel and Desmond; and Tom and Giana Ferguson – Gubbeen. All of these West Cork cheese pioneers first began producing their cheeses in 1978/9 but, in the decades that have followed, they have been joined by a veritable army of new Irish cheesemakers. An Irish cheese renaissance indeed!

Now, there are over nineteen cheesemakers in the county of Cork alone, with 61 per cent of all Irish cheese being made in Munster.

Some of these wonderful 'new' Cork cheeses include: Ardagh, Ardrahan, Ardsallagh, Carrigaline, Castlemary, Cléire Goats, Clonmore, Coolea, Desmond, Gabriel, Durrus, St Gall, St Brigid Beag, Glenilen, Gubbeen, Hegarty's Cheddar, Milleens, Cáis Cruinn, Kilmichael and, last but by no means least, Toonsbridge Irish Buffalo Mozzarella.

If you are curious and would like to try some of these delicious cheeses, most are available from On The Pig's Back (stall 11) in the English Market.

On The Pig's Back

Stall 11

On The Pig's Back is a delicatessen-style stall selling hams, homemade pizza, Parma and Serrano ham, chorizo, merguez, freshly baked breads and the most comprehensive selection of Irish farmhouse cheeses in the Market. Choose from: Milleens, Hegarty's Cheddar, Ardrahan, Ardsallagh, Durrus, Gubbeen, St Tola and Triskel, to mention but a few. The staff at this stall are all very helpful and always tell customers that, if they don't have what you are looking for, they will get it.

Ballycotton Seafood

━━━━ ◆ ━━━━

Stall 40

The Walsh family began fishing out of Ballycotton Bay in East Cork over 20 years ago. Their dedication to supplying the freshest and best fish possible has seen their business grow year on year, from a small family business to an important local employer. They own their own fishing fleet and are proud to be able to guarantee the freshness of fish that they land and sell each day at their outlets around Cork and supply wholesale to the Irish food service industry from their processing plant in Garryvoe.

The Ballycotton Seafood stall in the English Market opened for business in January 2007 when the Bandon fish stall closed. The cheerful and ever-helpful Alan Wiggins manages the stall today with the help of Ivan Ellis, who had originally worked at the Bandon fish stall, and Wilfred Connan, a Frenchman who arrived in Ireland four years ago on a working holiday but is still here, having lost his heart to the English Market. 'Ballycotton Seafood employs fifty people on a full-time basis at the plant in Garryvoe,' says Alan, 'with that number increasing constantly as the demand for ready-prepared seafood dishes is growing year on year. We make our own fish pies, fish cakes, goujons and quiches and all the vegetables used in our products are supplied by local producers in Ballycotton. At our stall here in the English Market, shoppers can choose from at least forty different varieties of sea-fresh fish on any given day. We also have our own smokehouse and we produce top-quality smoked salmon and mackerel which are all hand sliced.'

Alan's top tips for recognising a good fresh fish are:
- The eyes should be clear, bright and slightly bulging.
- The gill should be bright red and have a seaweed odour.
- Every hour that a fresh fish is not on ice or well refrigerated, it loses one day's shelf life. So keep your fish well chilled.

Roast Haddock with Champ

Haddock is generally found in the North Atlantic and is a very popular fish, commonly used in the all-time classic 'fish and chips'.

Serves 4

4 x 175g/6oz skinless and boneless haddock fillets
salt and freshly ground black pepper
1 tbsp rapeseed oil
cherry tomatoes on the vine
25g/2oz butter
4 scallions, finely chopped
6 tbsp milk
900g/2lb freshly cooked floury potatoes, cut into even-sized chunks

Preheat the oven to 200°C/400°F/gas mark 6.

Arrange the haddock on a non-stick baking sheet and season, then drizzle over the rapeseed oil. Roast in the oven until cooked through and tender. Toss the tomatoes in a little oil and roast in the oven for 5 minutes.

Melt the butter in a small pan and gently sauté the scallions until softened. Pour in the milk and bring to a simmer. Mash the potatoes and then, using a wooden spoon, beat in the scallion and milk mixture until you have achieved a smooth, creamy mash. Season to taste. Divide the champ among warmed plates and arrange a piece of roasted haddock on each one to serve.

Try adding a little grated lemon rind or a crushed garlic clove to the fish fillets before drizzling with the rapeseed oil and roasting.
Other fish you could use for this recipe: whiting, hake or trout fillets.

Seared Ballycotton Scallops with Rashers of Bacon in an Irish Whiskey Cream Sauce

Scallops can be cooked in several different ways – stir-fry, grill, oven bake or fry – but they should not be cooked for long or they will become tough and lose their delicate flavour. One minute cooking time per side should be enough. Many people say that scallops should be cooked simply – a little garlic, a little butter – and very often that is all they need. However, for an extra-special starter, this recipe is worth trying; even if it is a little unorthodox to marry scallops with whiskey, the result is deliciously good. Scallops are in season from the end of July to the end of December.

Serves 4

12 scallops
2 scallions
150ml/5fl oz double cream
3 rashers of bacon
25ml/1 tbsp Irish whiskey
salt and pepper
8 scallop shells

Flash-fry the scallops in a little butter for 1 minute per side. Place them on a plate and put aside for later. Chop the scallions and fry in the same pan as the scallops. Remove the lightly fried scallions with a slotted spoon and put aside. Grill the bacon rashers and put aside to cool.

Place the same pan in which you have fried the scallops and scallions back on the heat, and when it is quite warm add the whiskey and set alight. Be very careful, as the flames can get quite high, but you have to burn off the alcohol or else the sauce will taste a little bitter. When the flame subsides, after about 5 seconds, add the cream, stir well and season with salt and pepper. Leave the sauce to simmer on a low heat for about 10 minutes until it has reduced by about half. Add the scallions.

Wash and dry the scallop shells. Cut the rashers into bite-sized pieces and add to the sauce. Put the cooked scallops into the clean shells, 3 scallops per shell, and pour the whiskey cream sauce over the scallop. Serve immediately, with 2 shells per person, or arrange the scallops on a nice serving dish.

Pan-Fried Hake with Lemon and Herb-Butter Sauce

Hake comes from the same family as cod and haddock. It is a small fish, averaging 1 to 8lb in weight, but has been known to grow up to 60lb. Hake can also grow up to 1 metre in length. Hake lives in shallow water, ranging in depth from 200 to 350m. Hake species stay in deep seawater during the day and come to the middle depths during the night.

Serves 4

4 x 175g/6oz hake fillets, skin on and boned
1 tbsp Irish rapeseed oil
salt and freshly ground black pepper
40g (about 2 tbsp) butter
1 tbsp chopped mixed herbs (parsley, chives and tarragon)
½ lemon, pips removed

Heat the oil in a large pan and add the seasoned hake fillets, skin-side down. Cook for a couple of minutes until the skin is just beginning to crisp, then add little knobs of butter to the pan around each hake fillet and cook for another couple of minutes until the skin is crisp.

Turn the hake fillets over and cook for another 3–4 minutes until cooked through. This will depend on the thickness of the fillets. Transfer to warmed plates while you make the sauce.

Add the rest of the butter to the frying pan and allow it to gently melt over a moderate heat. When it has melted, add a squeeze of lemon juice and the herbs, swirling the pan to combine. Season to taste. Spoon this sauce over the hake fillets and serve with steamed broccoli and some sautéed new potatoes.

Be careful not to overcook the fish. To check, gently prod the thickest part of the fish with a small knife. If it is cooked, the flesh will look opaque and the flakes will separate. If it is not done, the fish will still have the translucent look of raw fish. Other fish you could use for this recipe: whiting, haddock or trout fillets.

The Chocolate Shop

Stall P9

Niall and Rose Daly are passionate about chocolate. Together they run the stall known as The Chocolate Shop, tucked away on the left-hand side of the St Patrick Street exit of the Market. If you love chocolate, then a visit to this stall is a must. Niall and Rose source only the best-quality chocolate from around the world, including Valrhona, Amedi, Michel Cluzel, Domori, Callebaut and Willie's World Class Cacao, to mention but a few. A word of warning though – one look at the outstanding display of floor-to-ceiling chocolates and you'll be hooked, just like a big kid in a candy store! They also stock ranges of organic, gluten-free and diabetic chocolate, cooking chocolate, premium-quality drinking chocolate, nougat, marzipan, chocolate lollipops and the famous Cork brand of Hadji Bey's Turkish Delight. And if that wasn't enough, their famous 'chocolate shot' is not to be missed.

Niall and Rose also stock the popular Irish brand Cocoa Bean Chocolate Company, which includes interesting flavours such as Dark Chocolate with Chilli and Pink Peppercorn, Dark Chocolate with Gin and Tonic, and Milk Chocolate with Irish Honey.

The Skelligs Chocolate Company, which has been producing award-winning Irish chocolate for more than ten years, now also supplies Niall and Rose with gluten-free chocolate. Diabetic and low-carbohydrate chocolates are also available.

Rose Daly's Pear and Chocolate Tart

A decadent and luscious recipe for chocoholics. The refreshing pear cuts through the rich chocolate, resulting in . . . bliss. Serve with a dollop of lightly whipped cream or crème fraîche.

Serves 8–10

For the pastry
150g/4oz plain flour
pinch of salt
40g/1½oz icing sugar, and a little extra for dusting
85g/4oz unsalted butter, roughly cubed, and a little for greasing the tin
1 egg yolk

For the filling
2 eggs, separated
30g/1oz sugar
150ml/5fl oz milk
1 vanilla pod
200g/7oz real dark chocolate, finely chopped
3 large or 4 small ripe but firm pears, preferably Williams

To decorate and serve
fresh raspberries and 6 thin slices of pear
whipping cream, crème fraîche or vanilla ice-cream

To make the pastry, sift the flour, salt and icing sugar together. Rub in the butter until it resembles fine breadcrumbs. Add the egg yolk and mix together until combined. Wrap in clingfilm and chill for about 1 hour. Preheat the oven to 180°C/355°F/gas mark 4 and butter and flour the base and sides of a round loose-bottomed pie tin (4cm deep x 25cm diameter). Roll out the pastry and line the pie tin. Prick all over with a fork and bake blind, using baking beans and paper, for 15 minutes. Put to one side to cool.

To prepare the filling, beat the egg yolks and sugar in a heatproof bowl. In a separate pan, bring the milk and vanilla pod to the boil, then whisk the boiling milk into the egg mixture with a whisk. Keep whisking until the mixture thickens. Finally add the chopped chocolate and mix well (it will melt into the warm custard mixture) to make the ganache.

Peel the pears, cut in half and scoop out the core and stem. Arrange the pear halves on the cooked pastry base. Whisk the egg whites in a clean bowl until forming soft peaks. Beat one-quarter into the custard, then fold the remainder in gently. Pour the mixture over the pears. Bake the tart for about 30 minutes, or until it has risen and set. Decorate with the raspberries and thinly sliced pear, and dust with icing sugar. Serve hot or cold, with whipped cream, crème fraîche or vanilla ice-cream.

English Market
Moist Chocolate Cake

All adults and children surveyed after trying this cake agreed unanimously that it was the best chocolate cake they ever tasted. Ever.

Serves 12–14

200g/7oz good-quality dark chocolate – about 60% cocoa solids
200g/7oz butter, cut into pieces
1 tbsp instant coffee granules
100g/3½oz self-raising flour
100g/3½oz plain flour
¼ tsp bicarbonate of soda
200g/7oz light muscovado sugar
25g/1oz cocoa powder
2 medium eggs
100ml/3½fl oz buttermilk

For the ganache
200g/7oz good-quality dark chocolate (same as above)
240m/8fl oz carton of pouring cream
2 tbsp castor sugar

Preheat the oven to 160°C/320°F/gas mark 3. Lightly grease two sandwich tins and line the bases with parchment paper. If you don't possess sandwich tins, then use a 20cm round cake tin (in this case, you will need to cook the cake for 1 hour 20 minutes).

Break the chocolate into a medium pan and add the butter. Mix the coffee granules with 25ml/1fl oz of cold water and add this to the pan also. Warm through over a low heat until everything is melted. Be careful not to overheat. Alternatively, melt the chocolate mixture in the microwave for about 4 minutes, but take it out and give it a stir after 2 minutes or else it might burn.

Mix the two flours, bicarbonate of soda, sugar and cocoa in a big bowl – make sure there are no lumps. Now, beat the eggs in a bowl and stir in the buttermilk.

Pour the chocolate mixture and the egg mixture into the flour and mix well. It should end up being quite a runny consistency. Divide the mixture between the two sandwich tins and cook in the centre of the oven for about 40 minutes. You can test with a skewer. Leave to cool in the tin (if you take it out too soon, it may crack as it is a moist cake, but you can always 'mend it' with the chocolate ganache). When the cakes are cold, tip them out on to a wire rack or a flat surface. If you are using the larger cake tin, cut it horizontally into three.

To make the ganache, chop the chocolate into small pieces and place in a bowl. Pour the cream into a pan, add the sugar, and heat until it is about to boil. Take off the heat and pour over the chocolate pieces. Stir until the chocolate has completely melted and the ganache is smooth.

Sandwich the cake layers together with a thin spread of the ganache. Pour the rest over the cake and let it fall down over the sides of the cake. Smooth it with a palette knife to cover all the sides. Leave to set for about 30 minutes (if you have that much willpower) and then decorate.

You can use a cheese slice to drag over a bar of white chocolate, which will create chocolate curls, and you can sprinkle these over the top. Or, you can decorate with milk chocolate and white chocolate buttons, with pretty coloured confectioners' flowers or fresh berries.

We recommend serving small slices, as this is a rich cake. We also recommend you serve this cake with whipped cream or ice-cream to counterbalance the chocolate.

This cake keeps very well for several days in a sealed container. In fact, it is even better on the second day, when it has had time to 'mature'.

Hadji Bey's Turkish Delight Ice-Cream Terrine

Who would have thought that 'Turkish Delight' and 'Cork' could be so inextricably linked? But they are. Ask any Corkonian what Hadji Bey means to them, and they will be transported back to floral quivering squares of Turkish Delight dusted in icing sugar.

It all began in the early 1900s, when an Armenian immigrant by the name of Harutun Batmazian arrived in Cork. The International Exhibition of 1903 was about to take place – a huge event for Cork at the time. The story goes that Harutun decided to set up a stall making and selling Turkish Delight, as he thought it might be a popular treat for visitors to the city. His stall proved to be a resounding success, enabling the young Armenian to set up shop on MacCurtain Street, which subsequently became a well-known Cork landmark.

Sadly, the shop closed when Harutun's son Eddie retired in the 1970s, but recently LC Confectionery began re-making the delicacy and packaging it in boxes that replicate the original. Now you can buy Hadji Bey's Turkish Delight (made from the original recipe) at The Chocolate Shop in the English Market.

Serves 8
Makes a 1-litre/1¾ pint terrine
Begin this recipe a day in advance – it is very easy to make, and well worth trying

a little vegetable oil, for brushing on to the clingfilm to ensure easy removal
enough cling film to line a 1-litre loaf tin

800g fresh ricotta, from the cheese counter
165g/5oz caster sugar
300ml/½ pint double cream
125g/4oz shelled unsalted pistachio nuts
250g/9oz Hadji Bey's Turkish Delight
2 tbsp rosewater (available at Mr Bell's)

For the rose syrup
200g/7oz caster sugar
1 tbsp rosewater
a few drops of rose food colouring

Line a 1-litre terrine or loaf tin with clingfilm and lightly grease the clingfilm with a little vegetable oil. Leave some clingfilm overhanging the sides of the tin.

In a large bowl, beat the ricotta and sugar until smooth. In another bowl, whip the cream to soft peaks then gently fold into the ricotta mixture, keeping as much air in the mixture as possible. Fold in the pistachios, Turkish delight and rosewater.

Fill the terrine with the ricotta mixture, packing it down firmly. Cover with the overhanging clingfilm and freeze overnight until firm.

To make the rose syrup, heat the sugar and 250ml/9fl oz water in a small pan over a low heat. Stir until dissolved. Bring to the boil, then simmer for 5 minutes until the syrup thickens. Cool the syrup, then add the rosewater to taste. Add a few drops of food colouring until you have the desired 'pinkness'.

Remove the terrine from the freezer 10 minutes before serving, to soften. Unwrap the top and turn out on to a serving plate. Slice, and drizzle with the rose syrup just before serving.

Strawberries Dipped in Chocolate

For the easiest and quickest of all chocolate dessert treats, just dip some strawberries in a little melted chocolate and leave to set on parchment paper for a couple of minutes before serving. Children love these simple little delicious treats.

The History of
Milleens Cheese

'When Veronica Steele first started making cheese in 1976 it is sure she did not realise that twenty-five years later it would be known as the cheese where the story of modern Irish farmhouse cheesemaking begins. Milleens is an artisan food, a washed rind cheese with a soft paste. It has a mottled peach and sometimes fiery orange washed rind and within this is a paste that goes from semi-firm to spilling cream. The flavour is a complex mix of delicate herbs along with a spicy tang. Available in 1.5kg and 200g rounds, the smaller known as "dotes".'

Bord Bia, *Sourcing Irish Farmhouse Cheese*

The following piece is Veronica's account of how she came to be one of Ireland's first pioneer cheesemakers and how she happened upon her recipe for her beloved Milleens cheese.

The origin of the initial concept is fading in the mists of time. Hunger and shame. There was nothing to eat! Nothing interesting. The old shop in Castletownbere with its saucepans and shovels and Goulding's Manures, clock wagging away the time, and smoked hams hanging from hooks in the ceiling, and huge truckles of cheddar on the wooden counter with their mouldy bandages and the crumbs of the cheese strewn around, scrumptious, tempting, melt-in-the-mouth crumbs which you could nibble at as you queued to be served, with your message list. And then she would cut a fine big chunk, golden or white, and what I missed the most was the way it crumbled.

So they closed it and gutted it and extended it and reopened it. Enter the trolley. Spotless, sterile, pre-packed portions sweating in their plastic. Tidy piles. Electronic scales. Keep moving. Don't block the aisles. No idle chatter. Big brother is watching you. Don't ask for credit. Oh boy!

And then one day in a different shop that jolly French pair of geriatrics asking for the local cheese and being given Calvita.

And then we bought a farm and a cow. Her name was Brisket and she only had one horn. She lost the other one gadding down a hill, tail-waving, full of the joys of spring. Her brakes must have failed. We had to put Stockholm tar on the hole right through the hot summer. And all the milk she had. At least three gallons a day. Wonder of wonders and what to do with it all. And then remembering those marvellous cheddars. So for two years I made cheddars. They were never as good as the ones in Castletownbere had been, but they were infinitely better than the sweaty vac-packed bits. Very little control at first but each failed batch spurred me on to achieve. I was hooked. Once I had four little cheddars on a sunny windowsill outside, airing themselves, and Prince, the dog, stole them and buried them in the garden. They were nasty and sour and over-salted anyway. Those were the days.

So one day Norman said, 'Why don't you try making a soft cheese for a change.' So I did. It was a quare hawk alright. Wild, weird and wonderful.

Never to be repeated. You can never step twice into the same stream for the first time. Now while this was all going on we had a mighty vegetable garden full of fresh spinach and courgettes and French beans and little peas, and all the sorts of things you couldn't buy in a shop for love nor money. And we would sell the superfluity to a friend who was a great chef in a restaurant and took great pains with her ingredients. She would badger the fishermen for the pick of their catch and come on a Monday morning with her sacks to root through our treasure trove of a garden for the freshest and the 'bestest'. Now, I was no mean cook myself and would have ready each Monday for her batches of yoghurt, plain and choc-nut, quiches, game pies (made with hare and cream – beautiful), pork pies, all adorned with leaves and rosettes as light and delicious as you can imagine, fish pies, and my speciality, gateau St Honoré – those were the days.

So there was this soft cheese beginning to run. We wrapped up about 12oz of it and away it went with the vegetables and the pies and all the other good things to Sneem and the Blue Bull restaurant, where it made its debut. Not just any old debut, because as luck would have it, guess who was having dinner there that very same night? Attracted no doubt by Annie's growing reputation and being a pal of the manager's, Declan Ryan of the Arbutus Lodge Hotel in Cork had ventured forth to sample the delights of Sneem, and the greatest delight of them all just happened to be our humble cheese. The first, the one and only, Irish Farmhouse Cheese. At last the real thing after so long. Rumour has it that there was a full eclipse of the sun and earth tremors when the first Milleens was presented on an Irish cheeseboard.

The product had now been tested and launched. Its performance post-launch left nothing to be desired. The very next night, Ms Myrtle Allen, accompanied no doubt by other family members of Ballymaloe House, also engaged in testing the waters of Sneem, polished off the last sliver of the wonderful new cheese and was impressed by its greatness. And the rest, as they say, is history. Those were the days.

Veronica Steele

The Farmer

Stall 30a

Michael Hurley runs a stall called 'The Farmer' which specialises in premium-quality fresh fruit, vegetables, duck eggs and free-range eggs. Many people complain that fresh figs are difficult to come by after the summer months, but Michael always seems to have a plentiful supply. 'When it's winter here, it's summer somewhere else, so we can usually get hold of them all year round', says Michael.

Michael set up the stall twenty years ago when his farm in Mallow ran into financial difficulty. Luckily for him, his family all rallied around and were able to secure a stall for him in the English Market. He hasn't looked back since. For the past sixteen years he has been assisted by employee and friend, Ann Sexton. Michael is able to do deliveries, whilst Ann runs the stall.

Before the Queen's historic visit to Cork and to the English Market in 2011, Michael said he hardly gave the whole event a second thought. 'I thought the Queen would come and would leave and that would be that,' he says. 'I thought I wouldn't even catch a glimpse of her; there was so much commotion in the Market in the lead-up to the visit.' But when the Queen actually stopped at Michael's stall and chatted to him he was totally unprepared for the effect that this would have on him. 'I felt really honoured and privileged to have met her. You can tell that she really is a very genuine and kind person.'

In fact, this sentiment was echoed by many Cork people. 'In the few days she spent as a guest of our country, her smile lit up the whole nation and we felt great affection and admiration for her, certainly a reaction which nobody could have foreseen or predicted,' says Michael.

Michael now proudly displays a large framed photograph of himself with the Queen on the wall of his stall. 'Who would ever have thought that the Queen of England would visit Michael Hurley's fruit and vegetable stall in the English Market in Cork?' Michael asks. Who indeed?

English Market Vegetable Soup

Delicious, nutritious and filling. You can make this recipe a day in advance or even freeze it so you'll always have a great soup at hand when you are too busy to cook. Both vegetarians and carnivores give this recipe the thumbs-up.

Serves 4–6

a little oil to sauté the vegetables
1 onion, diced
3 carrots, sliced
2 bell peppers, one red, one green
3 celery stalks, finely chopped
3 garlic cloves, minced
3 cups green cabbage, diced
½ tsp dried oregano
1 tsp coriander seeds
1 tsp basil
½ tsp salt
1½ litres chicken stock
3 medium potatoes, peeled and chopped
parsley, chopped for serving

In a large pot heat the olive oil. Add in all the vegetables except the potatoes. It is important not to add the potatoes at this stage, as the starch in them will cause them to stick and burn at the bottom of the pot.

Add the seasoning, basil, oregano and coriander seeds. Continue to turn the vegetables over a low heat until you can see moisture gathering in the bottom of the pot. Add the stock, followed by the potatoes. Bring to the boil and reduce to a simmer. Depending on how small you have cut the vegetables, the soup should take 20–30 minutes to cook.

Remove from the heat once all the vegetables are soft and easily crushed with a fork. Pour off a little of the liquid and set aside. This is the best way to control how thick or thin your soup is.

Pour the remaining vegetables and stock into a blender. Once the soup has been puréed and poured through a strainer, you can correct the seasoning and consistency by adding the liquid you saved if it is too thick. Before serving, finish with the chopped parsley.

Blackberry and Apple Crumble

Blackberry and apple crumble is comfort food at its best. This Irish country farmhouse dessert is very easy to prepare. Serve with whipped cream, ice-cream or custard for an indulgent autumnal experience . . .
'Season of mists and mellow fruitfulness' – John Keats.

Serves 6–8

675g/1½ lb Bramley apples, peeled, cored and chopped
55g/2oz sugar
2 tbsp water
50g/2oz (about 10–12) blackberries

For the crumble
55g/2oz butter
90g/4oz white flour
55g/2oz caster sugar

Preheat the oven to 180°C/350°F/gas mark 4. Stew the apples gently with the water in a covered casserole dish for 5–10 minutes until slightly softened. Taste and add more sugar if you would like the fruit to be sweeter. Pour the half-stewed fruit into a 1.1-litre/2-pint pie dish and allow to cool. Meanwhile, make the crumble.

Rub the butter into the flour until it begins to resemble breadcrumbs. Mix the sugar into this butter and flour mixture.

Sprinkle the blackberries over the apple mixture and then cover the fruit with the crumble mixture. Bake in the oven for 30–45 minutes until golden brown.

O'Sullivan's Poultry

Glenys Landon & Daughters

Stall P10

Glenys Landon has been part of the English Market all her adult life. In recent years her daughters, Gwen and Daphne, have joined her in the business. Her stall is situated between the Princes Street end of the market and the exit to Patrick Street, where she trades under the name of O'Sullivan's Poultry. This was a stall steeped in Cork history and synonymous with the English Market in days gone by, so Glenys decided to keep the original name over the stall.

Glenys sells all types of poultry but also specialises in rarer cuts of meat, for instance kangaroo fillets, ostrich fillets, guinea fowl, veal, pigeon, pheasant, duck, wild boar and rabbit, to mention but a few.

If you are looking to create a dish that is a little out of the ordinary, then Glenys has just the thing for you.

Her motto is 'The best fresh produce at the keenest prices'.

189

Fillets of Ostrich with Port and Cranberry Sauce

Ostrich meat is a red meat that is low in fat and can be used in any traditional red-meat recipe to produce great-tasting dishes – the secret is not to overcook it. Because of the lack of fat, this meat cooks quickly, shrinks very little, but may dry out if overcooked.

Serves 4

375ml/16fl oz red wine
2 tbsp cranberry jelly
125ml/4fl oz port
100ml/3½ fl oz fresh cream
800g ostrich steaks, 2 thin steaks per person
2 tbsp olive oil
1 tbsp crushed black peppercorns
4 tbsp whole green peppercorns
4 sprigs fresh rosemary

Pour the red wine into a saucepan and bring to the boil over a medium heat. Stir in the cranberry jelly. Reduce the heat and simmer for about 10 minutes. Add the port and reduce again until the sauce is quite thick. Finally add the cream and leave to reduce for a few minutes more.

Brush the steaks with a little oil (they are so lacking in fat that you actually have to add some) and then place them on a plate containing the crushed black peppercorns and whole green peppercorns. Cover each side of the steaks in peppercorns. Heat a little oil in a frying pan over a medium to high heat, place the steaks into the pan and cook quickly for 2 minutes per side.

When the steaks are cooked, arrange on plates, one wedged slightly on top of the other. Add the juice of the pan to the sauce, stir and pour over the steaks. Decorate with sprigs of rosemary.

Serve with vegetables of your choice.

Kangaroo Fillet with Sweet Parsnips

Kangaroo has always been a source of food for indigenous Australians. The meat is high in protein and low in fat (only about 2 per cent). When compared with other foods, kangaroo meat has a very high concentration of conjugated linoleic acid (CLA). CLA has been attributed with a wide range of health benefits including having anti-carcinogenic and anti-diabetic properties, in addition to helping to reduce obesity and arteriosclerosis.

Kangaroo meat has a slightly stronger flavour than other meats, but it is quite tender and tastes similar to a good beef steak. It can be substituted in any dish that would normally call for beef or lamb.

Serves 4

4 tomatoes
400ml natural yoghurt
200ml vinaigrette dressing
375ml jar Tandoori marinade
4 kangaroo tenderloin fillets, about 60 grams each
2 large handfuls of salad leaves
2 parsnips
150ml olive oil
salt and black pepper

This dish consists of a stack of dressed baby salad leaves topped with thin strips of kangaroo tenderloin fillet, which has been marinated in yoghurt and tandoori marinade spices and then pan-fried. The accompaniment is thin-cut, deep-fried parsnip.

First see to the dressing. Purée the tomatoes in a blender (or with a fork), add the vinaigrette dressing and then whisk together. Put to one side until the dish is ready to serve.

Mix the yoghurt with the tandoori marinade. Marinate the kangaroo tenderloin fillets in this mixture in the refrigerator for about 4 hours. Add 2 tablespoons of oil and salt and pepper to the marinade, then cook the fillets quickly on a high heat in a well-oiled frying pan for about 5 minutes. Leave the meat to rest on a plate covered in foil for a further 5 minutes.

While the meat is resting, wash the salad leaves and arrange in a pile on each plate. Peel then slice the parsnips lengthwise and then deep-fry them for 5 minutes or until golden brown. Slice the kangaroo fillets in half, and then cut into long strips and arrange randomly across the stack of salad leaves on the plate with the slices of parsnip. Dress all the ingredients with the tomato vinaigrette dressing and serve immediately.

Roast Garlic Quails Wrapped in Parma Ham

Perfect for a dinner party starter – something a little out of the ordinary.

Serves 4

3 garlic bulbs, unpeeled
4 small sprigs rosemary
4 quails (1 per person)
40g/2oz butter, slightly softened
salt and freshly ground black pepper
4 slices Parma ham
50ml/2fl oz sweet Madeira
350ml/16fl oz chicken stock

Heat the oven to 200°C/390°F/gas mark 6. Divide 2 garlic bulbs into separate cloves and place a clove (unpeeled) and a sprig of rosemary inside the cavity of each quail. Halve the remaining 3 bulbs of garlic horizontally and place in a large roasting dish. Smear the butter over each quail breast and season with a little salt and pepper.

Wrap each bird in a slice of Parma ham and place in the large roasting tin with the halved garlic bulbs. Use 2 tins if necessary – don't pack the quails in too tightly or they may not cook properly. Roast in the oven for 35–40 minutes.

Remove the quails to a serving plate and keep warm. Press down on the halved garlic bulbs in the roasting tin using a spoon to extract the pulp.

Place a saucepan over a medium heat and add the Madeira and the garlic pulp. Cook to reduce a little, and then add the chicken stock. Simmer for 3–4 minutes, then pass all the liquid through a sieve, squashing the garlic to extract as much flavour as possible. Discard the garlic skins.
Taste and season with a little salt and pepper.

Pour the sauce over or around the quails and serve with watercress salad and baby roast potatoes.

The Sandwich Stall

Stall 39

This a very attractive stall, which has retained part of its predecessor's original stall features. The original stall was M. & E. Sheehan's, a fishmongers, which began trading in 1906 and ceased trading in the late 1990s.

Now, coffee, refreshments, gourmet sandwiches, homemade soups and salads are freshly prepared at the Sandwich Stall each morning in time for the busy lunchtime rush.

Ashley O'Neill

Stalls 35 & 36

Ashley O'Neill comes from a long line of master butchers dating back to 1922. As a young boy he served his apprenticeship at his uncle's shop in Turner's Cross. However, the young Ashley had an urge to travel and took a job on board the *Queen Mary*, where he worked his way around the world as a butcher. Subsequently, he worked on board the *Queen Elizabeth*, but after ten years on the high seas Ashley felt that he had seen enough and returned home to his native Cork, where he opened his own shop in the English Market in 1976. All of Ashley's meat is locally sourced; he sells beef, lamb, pork and a small amount of poultry, as well as eggs. Ashley's eggs must come from very happy hens as they are remarkably large and very frequently double-yoked.

Ashley suggests that you should always allow your meat to come to room temperature (this takes about 20 minutes) before cooking and always allow at least 10 minutes resting time before carving. Resting helps the meat to achieve full flavour and tenderness. Cover the meat with foil and leave it to rest in a warm place for about 10 minutes. It also helps if the dinner plates are hot as, if you serve your meat on cold plates, the meat will become cold quickly.

Ashley accepts orders by telephone: 021 4270535.

Ashley O'Neill's Rib-Eye Steak on a Red Wine Reduction with Balsamic Onions, Wild Mushrooms and Hand-Cut Potato Chips

Cooking smaller cuts of meat can be a challenge, even for experienced chefs, as smaller cuts tend to dry out and become tough if cooked too quickly. A good heavy frying pan or griddle can help to reduce the risk of the meat becoming leathery or tough.

Serves 4

4 rib-eye steaks
1 tbsp ground black pepper
sea salt, a good pinch per steak to season
½ tbsp Irish rapeseed oil
55g/2oz butter
4 medium onions
30ml/3 tbsp balsamic vinegar
225g/8oz wild mushrooms (available at the Good Food Shop, stall 28)

First of all, see to the red wine reduction
For the red wine reduction see the Bubble Brothers' recipe on page 68.

Next, see to the chips
800g/1½lb potatoes or 2 medium-sized potatoes per person
2 litres/3 pints Irish rapeseed oil

Peel the potatoes and cut them into 1cm rounds, then cut each round into 3–4 chips, depending on how thick you want your chips to be. Spread out the chips on a clean tea towel, then pat dry with some kitchen paper. Line a baking tray with a double layer of kitchen paper.

Pour the rapeseed oil into a large deep pan. Make sure that it is no more than a quarter full. If it is too full, the oil will overflow when you add your chips. You don't want that to happen. Heat the oil to 160°C (moderately hot) or when a cube of bread turns brown after 1 minute of frying.

Carefully add a couple of handfuls of chips to the pan and cook for 4–5 minutes, stirring occasionally so that they don't stick together. At this stage, they will be soft but not golden. Remove with a slotted spoon and transfer to the baking tray which you have lined with kitchen paper. Repeat the process until all the chips have had their first immersion. (It takes two immersions in the oil to fully cook the chips, firstly at a moderate heat of 160°C, then, for a second immersion, quite hot at 190°C). *For the time being, take the oil off the heat and leave the chips to one side until after the steaks have been cooked.*

Next see to the onions and mushrooms

Prepare and slice the onion and mushrooms. Fry the mushrooms in a large heavy-based frying pan with a generous knob of butter. A minute should be sufficient, as you will be putting them in the oven covered with foil on a heatproof serving dish to keep warm until ready to serve, and they will continue to cook there.

Cook the onions in the same way, but add the balsamic vinegar when the onions begin to turn golden; stir in and leave to simmer for 2–3 minutes. Remove to a serving dish, cover with foil and place in the oven to keep warm with the mushrooms.

To cook the steaks

Allow the steaks to come to room temperature (about 20 minutes). Preheat a heavy frying pan or griddle – it should be hot but not smoking, otherwise the meat will burn on the outside before the inside has time to cook. However, if the pan is too cold, the steaks will be tough. (No pressure then!) Brush the steaks with oil (to avoid using too much) or pour a little in the pan if you prefer. Season the steaks well with black pepper and sea salt.

The approximate cooking times for a 2.5cm (1 inch) thick steak are:

Rare: 1–2 minutes per side, rest for 6–8 minutes.
Medium rare: 2–2½ minutes per side, rest for 5 minutes.
Medium: 3 minutes per side, rest for 4 minutes.
Well done: 4½ minutes per side, rest for 1 minute.

Remember, resting the steaks allows the meat to become moist and tender all the way through. Rest the steaks on a warm plate in a warm area of the kitchen, covered in foil. Only follow the next step when the steaks have been cooked and you are almost ready to sit down.

Finishing off the chips

Heat the oil so that it is hotter for the second immersion. It should be at least 190°C. When it has reached this temperature (or when a cube of bread turns brown after 20–30 seconds), cook the chips for the second time. Once they are golden brown, they will be ready to be served immediately with a sprinkling of sea salt.

Serve up the steaks on warm plates with a portion of mushrooms, onions, chips and a little red wine reduction.

Leg of Lamb with Parsley, Rosemary and Garlic

What could be more delicious than Irish grass-fed lamb? Though great at any time of year, this comforting Sunday roast is best enjoyed with family and friends in winter. The most important thing to remember when roasting a leg of lamb is not to over cook it. Lamb should be roasted for twenty minutes per 450g/1lb, plus an extra twenty minutes.

Serves 6–8

1 leg of lamb
1 tsp fresh thyme leaves, chopped
1 tsp fresh rosemary, chopped
2 cloves of garlic, chopped
30ml/1fl oz Irish rapeseed oil
sea salt and black pepper

Take the lamb out of the fridge and allow it to reach room temperature before placing it in a roasting dish. Make small incisions along the top of the joint with a sharp knife – about ten to twenty incisions should suffice. Mix the herbs, garlic and oil in a bowl and pour over the lamb, allowing it to settle into the incisions. Season well with sea salt and black pepper.

To cook:

Preheat the oven to 200°C/gas mark 6. Cook at 200°C/gas mark 6 for the first twenty minutes and then reduce to 170°C/gas mark 4 for the remainder of the cooking time. When the lamb is cooked to your liking, cover it with foil and allow it to rest for fifteen to twenty minutes before carving.

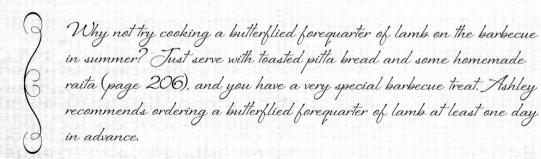

Why not try cooking a butterflied forequarter of lamb on the barbecue in summer? Just serve with toasted pitta bread and some homemade raita (page 206), and you have a very special barbecue treat. Ashley recommends ordering a butterflied forequarter of lamb at least one day in advance.

Cucumber and Mint Raita

Serves 6

250ml natural yoghurt
½ cucumber, grated or finely chopped
handful of mint leaves, chopped
large pinch of sea salt
½–1 green chilli, deseeded and finely chopped

Wrap the grated cucumber in a tea towel and squeeze out any excess water. Mix all the ingredients together and serve chilled.

The
Real Olive Company

Stall 33

Established in 1994, this stall provides shoppers with the best in olives, olive oils, chillies, feta cheese, sun-dried tomatoes, stuffed vine leaves and generally all the culinary delights of the Mediterranean.

Turkey for Christmas

By Mairéad Lavery,
Editor of Irish Country Living, *The Farmers' Journal.*

Turkeys – when I think of them it's never an image of the splendid bird on the Christmas table that comes to mind. Instead they evoke memories of growing up on a farm in Wicklow and rearing turkeys from the time they were day-olds.

We'd get the 150 turkey chicks from a hatchery in Carlow and have a corner of the trap-loft ready for them. Surrounded by boxes, with a warm timber floor, infra-red lamp, food pellets and an upturned jam jar of water, they were in the lap of luxury.

When they were tiny we'd go and play with them. If you sat on the floor they'd all come running and you'd have them on your lap and around your feet, and if you stayed still they would all just snuggle into you and go to sleep.

In no time they'd outgrow the trap-loft and be moved to a bigger house down the yard. The turkeys were always let out to graze for much of the day and, as children, it was our job to get them back into their house before dusk. Of course, some evenings we'd forget and then we'd have a right job getting them down from the trees where they'd take roost.

Come the second week of December, my mother would start organising the boiler house where the turkeys were to be killed and plucked. This was adults' work, but there was plenty for us children to do as well.

To make sure the turkeys looked their best for the sales we'd have to clean their feet and legs, tidy the wing feathers and remove all the pin feathers from the breast and legs. It was slow, painstaking work and it was all done in the house, so there would be turkeys everywhere.

Of course those were the days when we had no central heating, so there was no fear of them going 'off' in the Siberian temperatures of the dining room.

We sold the turkeys at a mart in Ashford and the night before we'd load up and set out at about 3am to travel the 20 miles or so. We'd have sandwiches, flasks of tea, a couple of quilts and hot jars, because selling turkeys was a marathon job.

You might ask why we'd be heading off at that unearthly hour, but there was a logic to it. You see, it was really important to have a good place in the queue for the mart. Too near the top and there wouldn't be enough buyers competing with each other to get you a decent price. Too far down the queue and you'd find that half the buyers were already on the road home.

So we'd pull in to the car park of one of the pubs that faced the mart and wait until the first cars made their move. As soon as a queue began to form, cars appeared from everywhere looking to get the best spots and then we waited, sometimes for up to ten hours, before the auctioneer's hammer fell to mark the end of turkeys for another year.

Yes, when I think of turkey, it's never the image of the splendid bird on the Christmas table that comes to mind.

P. Coughlan

Stall 31

P aul Murphy qualified as a butcher at the age of sixteen in 1960; he had been the ripe old age of eleven when he first began to work in the Market. Paul's great-grandmother (on his mother's side) first started the business over a century ago when she took a stall on Cornmarket Street towards the end of the 1940s. Her name was Lizzie Coughlan. Her son and grandson eventually took over the business but moved the stall indoors to the English Market. The English Market was made up mainly of butcher's stalls in the 1940s and '50s and Paul can remember over forty butchers trading there when he first started out as an apprentice butcher. Meat was hung from the rafters on large hooks and the floor was strewn with sawdust to absorb any 'spillages' which might occur as a result.

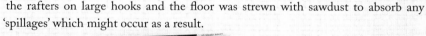

Today there are only eight butchers remaining in the English Market. This may be due in large part to changing trends in the grocery trade. At one time you could only buy meat from a butcher's shop, but nowadays you can buy meat in a supermarket or even from a local convenience store.

In the 1970s Paul remembers being approached by a salesman who tried to persuade him that 'refrigeration was the way forward'. Paul and all the other butchers thought he was crazy – nobody would ever buy meat from behind a glass-countered refrigeration unit! Would they? Today, that salesman is a good friend of Paul Murphy's and they both look back with nostalgia at the innocence of those

days. Glass-countered refrigeration units now purr contentedly at every second stall in the English Market.

In the 1980s Paul decided to branch out and he took another stall in the Market; it specialised in health foods and vitamins. He also sold honey from West Cork and Wexford. In the 1990s he had a change of heart and decided to close the health-food stall and concentrate entirely on the meat side of his business. But as he had built up a loyal following for his honey products, he decided that he would continue to sell them. That is the reason that Paul now sells premium-quality meats *and* honey.

Of all the meat cuts, a historic speciality of Coughlan's which is currently enjoying a revival and which was very popular in times gone by is corned mutton. Perhaps Paul has HRH the Prince of Wales to thank for this renewed interest in mutton as the Prince instigated a movement called The Mutton Renaissance Campaign in 2004. The campaign received the backing of the Academy of Culinary Arts (of which the Prince is patron) to get mutton back on the menu in the UK. It appears that the campaign has been a success. Mutton is now back in favour and served in some of the finest restaurants in both the United Kingdom and Ireland. Moreover, it appears regularly on the menu of the Farmgate Restaurant, which is situated in the upstairs gallery of the Market, and the mutton is supplied by Paul Coughlan.

Paul's son Alan is now a partner in the business, the fifth generation to enter into the meat trade. Lizzie Coughlan would be proud.

Leg of Salted Mutton with a Caper Sauce

Paul Coughlan's twenty-first-century recipe for preparing corned mutton.

Serves 6–8

2 bay leaves,
2 onions, roughly chopped
2 carrots, roughly chopped
2 sticks of celery, roughly chopped
350ml/½ pint chicken stock
1 leg of corned mutton

Place the peeled and roughly chopped vegetables and bay leaves in a large saucepan. Cover the vegetables with the chicken stock and then add the leg of mutton. Add more cold water to the pot until the mutton is covered in liquid. Bring the saucepan to the boil and then reduce the heat immediately so that the mutton cooks at a simmer for a further 1¾ hours.

For the caper sauce
50g/2oz butter
50g/2oz flour
300ml/½ pint of milk
300ml/½ pint of stock (taken from the mutton pot)
a generous handful of parsley, chopped
2 tbsp of capers, chopped
salt and ground black pepper

Melt the butter in a saucepan, add the flour and stir in to make a roux. Slowly add the milk, stirring all the time until the sauce resembles a thin cream. You may need to whisk the sauce for a minute or two to make sure there are no lumps. Finally, add the stock, parsley and capers. Season with salt and black pepper. Serve poured over the mutton with seasonal vegetables and floury spuds.

Corned Beef and Parsnip Mash with Irish Mustard and Cider Sauce

Even if you think you are not a real fan of corned beef, Paul urges you to give this recipe a try.

Serves 6

2kg/5lb silverside or brisket corned beef
1 carrot
2 celery sticks
2 leeks
1 tsp black or white peppercorns
250ml/9fl oz dry cider

For the parsnip mash
½ kg/1lb potatoes, peeled and chopped
½ kg/1lb parsnips, peeled and chopped
125ml/4fl oz mixture of milk and cream
knob of butter
salt and black pepper

Irish mustard and cider sauce
50g/2oz butter
25g/1oz flour
1 tbsp mustard
100m/3½fl oz cooking liquid (the water the meat has been cooked in)
100ml/2½fl oz dry cider
dash of cream
2 tbsp scallions, chopped

Place the joint in a large saucepan. Add the chopped vegetables, peppercorns and cider. Add enough water to cover the joint. Bring to the boil, then simmer for approximately 40 minutes per ½kg/1lb or until the meat is tender.

Leave in the liquid until ready to serve. While the meat is cooking, place the potatoes and parsnips in a large pot. Cover with water. Season, bring to the boil, then simmer until both parsnips and potatoes are cooked. Drain well, then mash really well with the milk, cream and butter. Season well. Keep warm.

To make the sauce, melt the butter and stir in the flour. Cook for a minute or two. Add the mustard and whisk in the cooking liquid and cider. Bring to the boil, then simmer for 3–4 minutes. Stir in the cream and scallions and taste for seasoning. Serve the corned beef sliced with the parsnip mash, sauce and some buttery cabbage.

The following is a recipe taken from the classic Victorian cookbook *Mrs Beeton's Book Of Household Management* and gives us an idea of how our ancestors went about preparing similar cuts to those we cook today.

Mrs Beeton's Book of Household Management (1861)

ROAST HAUNCH OF MUTTON

726. INGREDIENTS.—Haunch of mutton, a little salt, flour.

Mode.—Let this joint hang as long as possible without becoming tainted, and while hanging dust flour over it, which keeps off the flies, and prevents the air from getting to it. If not well hung, the joint, when it comes to table, will neither do credit to the butcher nor the cook, as it will not be tender. Wash the outside well, lest it should have a bad flavour from keeping; then flour it and put it down to a nice brisk fire, at some distance, so that it may gradually warm through. Keep continually basting, and about ½ hour before it is served, draw it nearer to the fire to get nicely brown. Sprinkle a little fine salt over the meat, pour off the dripping, add a little boiling water slightly salted, and strain this over the joint. Place a paper ruche on the bone, and send redcurrant jelly and gravy in a tureen to table with it.

Time.—About 4 hours. Average cost, 10d. per lb. Sufficient for 8 to 10 persons.

Seasonable.—In best season from September to March.

Lavender Custard with West Cork Honey and Berries

Something a little out of the ordinary for dessert; it's like taking a stroll through a forest on a summer's day.

Serves 6

250ml/9fl oz milk
5 eggs yolks and 1 whole egg
125g/4oz caster sugar
250ml/9fl oz double cream
1 tbsp fresh or dried lavender flowers without the stem
drizzle of honey

Put the lavender flowers in a pan with the milk. Bring to the boil slowly then take off the heat and leave to stand for 5–10 minutes so that the flavour can infuse.

Whisk all 5 egg yolks and the whole egg with the caster sugar until pale and thick. Pour the milk through a strainer or sieve so as to catch the lavender flowers. Whisk the milk into the egg mixture and transfer to a clean saucepan. Return the saucepan to a medium heat and stir continuously until the custard thickens.

Stir in the cream, and serve with fresh berries and a drizzle of honey.

The Good Food Shop

Stall 28

Marc O'Mahony opened his stall called The Good Food Shop in 1999. Marc was originally an organic market gardener and supplied shops and stalls with organic produce from his own garden in Rossmore in West Cork. However, Marc found that he was increasingly spending more and more time on the road doing deliveries and less and less time where he wanted to be – in his garden. As demand for organic produce was growing steadily during the late 1990s, Marc's solution was to set up his own shop. That would leave him with only one outlet to supply (his own) and he would have more time for the gardening side of his business. As luck would have it, somebody told him that a stall in the English Market had become available; he applied for it and was successful.

The shop became busy after an initial slow start and customers were always enquiring about the different products. Marc discovered that somebody who was knowledgeable about the products had to be in the shop to answer customers' queries, and the best person for the job turned out to be Marc himself. So the end result is that Marc now spends most of his time working in the shop, and he buys his organic produce from his neighbours in West Cork.

'I've noticed recently that people seem to have gone back to the basics,' says Marc. 'Many of our customers have now started growing their own vegetables or herbs. I think many want to understand good food better and get closer to nature. They go out less to dinner and stay in to cook great, simple and wholesome food for themselves'.

223

'We take great pride in our seasonal local produce and stock things such as fresh purple sprouting broccoli in spring and we are the first to bring local gooseberries to market every summer. We do a great range of wild mushrooms in autumn and organic Brussels sprouts for Christmas!'

The Good Food Shop stocks an extensive range of flours, from teff to tapioca and corn to chestnut flour. There is also every imaginable spice, herb and various Irish seaweeds; a huge range of vegetarian **and vegan** foods as well as the full range of Green & Blacks chocolate for those **with a sweet** tooth.

The Good Food Shop delivers **next day** nationwide and can take orders by phone (021-4279419) or by email on marcomahony@hotmail.com.

Venison with Wild Mushrooms

The pairing of wild mushrooms and venison is a match made in heaven. If you like gamey, robust, earthy flavours and something a little out of the ordinary, then this recipe is surely worth trying.

Serves 4

a little oil
250g/9oz fresh wild mushrooms, sliced
1 clove of garlic, finely sliced
300g/11oz venison loin, trimmed and sliced into strips
   (available from Glenys Landon at O'Sullivan's Poultry stall, opposite the fountain)
salt and black pepper
15ml brandy
knob of butter
150ml crème fraîche

Heat a little oil in the pan and, over a medium heat, fry off the onions, mushrooms and garlic for about 5 minutes. Season the venison with salt and pepper and add to the onions, mushrooms and garlic, fry for a couple of minutes and then add the brandy, the knob of butter and the crème fraîche. Stir and leave to simmer on a very low heat for about 2 minutes. Venison will become tough if overcooked.

Serve on a bed of brown or basmati rice or with baby roast potatoes and seasonal vegetables.

Stir-fried Sprouts with Lemon and Pine Nuts

Brussels sprouts are a great source of folic acid and vitamin C. This recipe will change your mind about the much-maligned sprout.

Serves 4

600g/1½lb Brussels sprouts
1 tbsp oil (sesame seed oil works well here)
4 tbsp pine nuts
1 lemon, zest and juice
salt and pepper for seasoning

Cut away the bottom of the sprout and remove the outer leaves before cooking. Cut the sprouts in half. Cook the sprouts in boiling salted water for 3 minutes, then drain well.

Heat the oil in a wok or frying pan, then add the pine nuts and cook for about 30 seconds until the nuts begin to brown. Add the sprouts and the lemon zest and stir-fry for about 3 minutes. Finally add the lemon juice and season with salt and pepper.

Carrageen with Cream, Honey and Nutmeg

Carrageen (from the Irish, carrigín, 'little rock') is a species of red algae which grows abundantly along the Irish coastline. In many parts of the world it is known as 'Irish moss'. It is very rich in iron, iodine, fibre and anti-oxidants. Carrageen has a multitude of uses. It is commonly used as a thickener and stabiliser in dairy products such as ice-cream. In Europe it has an 'E' number of 407, so, if you see E407 in the ingredients of your ice-cream or other dairy desserts, you know that it contains carrageen. Traditionally in Ireland it is boiled in milk and strained, before sugar and other flavourings such as vanilla, cinnamon, brandy or whiskey are added. The end product is a kind of jelly similar to panna cotta, tapioca or blancmange. In this recipe the nutmeg, cream and honey combine with the carrageen mixture to give a treat that is unlike anything else.

Serves 4

a handful of carrageen (dried)
1 litre/1¾ pints full-fat milk
honey
fresh single cream
freshly grated nutmeg

Rehydrate the seaweed by soaking in water for 15 minutes. Pour the milk into a medium saucepan. Add the seaweed to the milk, gently heat and simmer for 30–45 minutes.

Pour the mixture through a sieve into a serving dish. Press the carrageen through the sieve so that it is puréed. Scrape all of it into the milk mixture and mix it thoroughly. You may have to use a whisk for this. Decant into individual glasses or bowls and chill in the fridge for a few hours until set.

Serve with generous portions of cream and honey and a sprinkling of freshly grated nutmeg.

Michael Bresnan
& Sons

Stall 5

Michael Bresnan's stall has the longest continuous family history in the English Market. Michael's grandfather had been an apprentice butcher in Castle Street when he decided to take his own stall in the Market in 1898. In 1908 he bought a farm, where he was able to rear his own livestock and, by doing so, ensure that he was able to supply his customers with top-quality produce. The Bresnan family farm is situated in the lush fields of Ballea, near Carrigaline, County Cork.

Today, the stall is run by the third generation of Bresnans. Michael's sons, Daniel, Neil and Peter, work with their father in the business that is now well over 100 years old. Michael and his sons continue the long family tradition of supplying premium produce, rearing, slaughtering and overseeing quality meat from field to fork. Michael Bresnan & Sons are members of the Master Meat Circle of Ireland, which guarantees that only local, wholesome, naturally produced and trusted quality meats are supplied to the consumer. Best animal husbandry practices are strictly adhered to and antibiotics and hormones are never used.

If you buy from a butcher who displays the Master Meat Circle of Ireland logo, you know that you are supporting generations of family-owned businesses, meat from your local area, local employment in the community, and tradition and skills that should be nurtured and supported for the survival of Irish master butchers. Michael's brother, Liam, also has a shop in Douglas Village.

Bresnan's Beef Casserole with Murphy's Stout

Michael suggests a hearty beef casserole. 'This is a terrific dish for a cold winter's day,' Michael says. 'It is comfort food at its best and will put a smile on your face, no matter how bad your day has been. It's absolutely historic.'

Serves 6

900g/2lb stewing beef, cut into 3cm/1 inch pieces
50g/2oz plain flour
salt and pepper
60ml Irish rapeseed oil
2 onions, roughly chopped
6 carrots, roughly chopped
2 cloves of garlic, finely chopped

2 tbsp tomato purée
1 litre/1¾ pints beef stock
500ml/18fl oz Murphy's stout
1 240g tin of chopped tomatoes
1 tbsp Worcestershire sauce
2 bay leaves
chopped fresh parsley, to garnish

Pat the beef dry with some kitchen paper. Stir the flour, salt and pepper in a bowl. Add the beef, turning to coat all the pieces, then shake off the excess flour and transfer to a plate.

Heat the oil in a large saucepan over a high heat. Brown the meat in two batches, turning occasionally, for about 5 minutes per batch. Transfer to a bowl.

Reduce the heat, add the onions and carrots to the saucepan and sauté for 10 minutes. Add the garlic and cook for 1 minute. Make sure to stir the bottom of the pot vigorously with a wooden spoon to deter any pieces from sticking to the pot. Add the tomato purée, stir to coat all of the vegetables and cook for about 1 minute more. Stir in all the beef. Add the beef stock, tin of tomatoes, Worcestershire sauce and bay leaves. Stir well. Bring the stew to the boil, then reduce the heat so the stew gently simmers. Continue to simmer, partially covered, for 1½–2 hours, stirring occasionally, until the beef is tender and the sauce has reduced and thickened.

Serve with crusty fresh bread.

You could also add a few peeled and quartered potatoes (or baby potatoes left whole, with their skins on) 40 minutes before the stew is due to be cooked. Place the potatoes on top of the stew and cover the pot for the last 40 minutes. Check the potatoes with a fork to make sure they are thoroughly cooked before serving.

Bresnan's Braised Beef with Buttery Mash and Turnip

An old family favourite, and a true taste of 'home'. Comforting, delicious, simple Irish homecooked beef, with none of the fuss and all of the flavour.

Serves 4–6

1.5kg/2½lb piece of braising beef, in one piece
a plate of seasoned flour
300g/11oz carrots, peeled and chopped
2 onions, chopped
1 swede turnip, peeled and diced
500ml/18fl oz beef stock

Preheat the oven to 180°C/355°F/gas mark 4. Cover the beef all over in the seasoned flour. In an oven-proof dish or roasting pan, heat a little of the oil and brown the beef on both sides. Then remove the beef and cover the onions, carrots and swede in the seasoned flour also. Add a little more oil to the dish or pan and fry off the vegetables for a couple of minutes. Place the beef on top of the vegetables and pour in the beef stock. Cover the dish with a lid or some tin foil and cook for 1½ hours. Then remove the lid and cook for a further hour at a lower heat, 160°C/320°F/gas mark 3.

For the buttery mash
1kg/2½lb floury potatoes, peeled, washed and cut into 2.5cm/1-inch chunks
salt and pepper
85g/3oz unsalted butter
225ml/8fl oz semi-skimmed milk, warmed

Simmer the potatoes in boiling salted water for 12–15 minutes. Drain, then cover with a clean tea towel to allow to 'dry out' for a couple of minutes. Mash the potatoes until smooth and season well with salt and pepper. Add the warm milk and butter and mix in well, then mash again until all the ingredients are well incorporated. Check the seasoning, adjust if necessary and serve immediately with the beef.

Bone Marrow with Boxty

Bone marrow has a strong meaty flavour and should be paired with a sauce which will create a balance of flavour, for example a caper and pine nut dressing or a salsa verde. Boxty is a very traditional Irish potato dish, which was eaten by the poorest of the poor, especially around the time of the Great Famine, and involves using all of the potato, skin included. Boxty (or in Irish bacstaí*) is a recipe also known as* Arán bocht tí, *which means 'poor house bread'. It has recently undergone a resurgence in popularity as interest in Irish food continues to gain momentum, is now served as a side dish, but it was once a staple in the diet of the poor.*

Serves 4

For the bone marrow
1 beef marrow bone cut into four 3-inch/8cm pieces
salt and freshly ground black pepper
a little oil for drizzling

For the caper and pine nut dressing
100ml/3½fl oz Irish rapeseed oil
1 shallot, finely chopped
1 garlic clove, crushed
2 tbsp pine nuts
1 tbsp capers
75ml/2½fl oz white wine vinegar
finely chopped parsley
sea salt and black pepper to season

Preheat the oven to 200°C/400°F/gas mark 6.

Place the bones on a baking sheet with the cutside facing upwards. Season with salt and freshly ground black pepper and drizzle with a little of the oil. Roast for about 20 minutes, or until the marrow comes away from the bone.

To make the dressing, heat the oil in a saucepan and fry the shallot and garlic for 2–3 minutes. Then add the pine nuts, capers, white wine vinegar and the remaining oil and cook for 3–4 minutes. Stir in the parsley and transfer to a serving dish.

For the boxty

Serves 4 as a side dish

500g potatoes (about 3 large potatoes)

60g butter, melted

handful of flour

generous grinding of sea salt and black pepper

little oil for frying

a handful of parsley, chopped

Clean the potatoes well and then grate them (unpeeled) on to a cloth that you have placed in the bottom of a bowl, so that all the grated potato lands on the cloth. Then hold up the cloth so that the starch and water will flow out of the grated potato and into the bowl. Squeeze the cloth so as to get all the liquid out. Discard the liquid.

Add the flour, salt and pepper to the grated potato and fry 4 spoonfuls of the mixture, the size of small pancakes, with a knob of melted butter in a pan. Each boxty should be about ¾ inch/2cm thick. Allow the base to brown nicely and then turn over to cook on the other side. Alternatively, you can fry the entire mixture as one large pancake and cut it into portions on serving.

Scoop out the marrow from each bone and spread on to the boxty, then top with the caper dressing and serve.

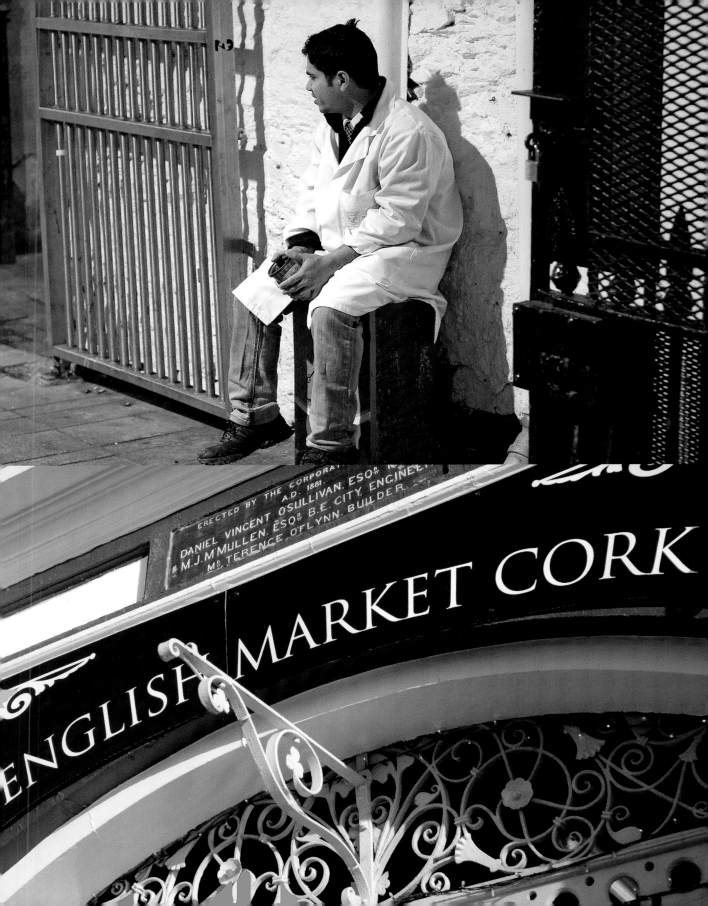

Spiced Beef

Nigel O'Mahony

Spiced beef: A cured and salted joint of rump or silverside beef, that is traditionally served at Christmas or the New Year in Ireland. This is a form of salt beef, cured with spices and saltpetre, and is usually boiled, broiled or semi-steamed in Guinness or a similar stout, and then sometimes roasted for a period afterwards. Varieties of spices used include pimento, cinnamon, ground cloves, ginger and black pepper.

So says Wikipedia. What do they know!

'Rump or silverside?' What about brisket or topside, or even rib? 'Cured and salted?' Surely 'corned and spiced' but would that be a wet spice or a dry? It all depends on who you talk to – but one thing is certain, if you do that talking in Cork, you'd better be in for a long and heated debate.

'The spice' is a closely guarded secret handed down from one generation to another – if they're deemed worthy. There's a reason for this. Spiced beef is a butcher thing – and anyone who knows anything about Cork butchers will tell you that, when they talk about meat, they aren't referring to sheep or pigs. Beef is king and treated with the respect given to royalty.

My father-in-law is a sixth-generation butcher. He retired with his spice recipe three years ago and spent six months working out which nephew to give it to. The other one hasn't spoken to him since. Last Christmas I asked him for it so I could try spicing my own. The reply was short: 'Get the brisket, I'll get it corned and then you're on your own!'

I did. He did as promised – and left me with three pink pieces of meat and a larder full of spice. I knew his recipe was a wet spice, so I decided to do a dry one – if it worked I could at least take the moral highground in that debate.

So on 1 December, I got the ground cloves, brown sugar, the salt, the mace, the cinnamon, the paprika and so on and mixed them together until the heady smell seemed familiar. I rubbed it all over the three joints of meat, placed them in a huge saucepan and put the pan in a cold larder.

Then every night until Christmas I checked them lovingly, turned them – and prayed for a result. While others were wrapping presents on Christmas Eve, I was rolling my spiced beef. It looked right, it felt right. As it gently came to a simmer in the pot, the whole house was filled with the scent of Christmas.

I left it to cool in the pot overnight and on Christmas morning my father-in-law was given the honour of cutting and taking the first taste. 'Not bad, Nigie,' he said. 'What spices did you put in it?

You get the same answer that he got: 'That's for me and the next six generations to know!'

Healy's Bakery

Stall 2

H ealy's Bakery is Cork's oldest surviving bakery and will celebrate its 150th year in business in 2012. The business was initially established by Michael Healy in 1862, who operated from his premises on the Grand Parade, a stone's throw away from the English Market. The business thrived under Michael's watchful eye, but his son Tom (whom he had intended leaving it to) had gone to England and joined the British army. Michael, believing his son had settled in England, accepted an offer on the bakery from his friend and neighbour Henry O'Shea and sold the business as a going concern. Two years later, O'Shea was having problems running the business and asked Michael if he would consider running it for him. Bored, after two years of leading a life of leisure, Michael Healy was delighted to return to the business of making bread and so agreed to run the business for his neighbour.

However, shortly after embarking on his new career path as an employee in his former business, Michael's son Tom returned home from England, eager to learn the ropes of the family bread-making business. This prompted his father to spring into action. His solution? Start up another bakery, which his son Tom would run. And so, Healy's Bakery in Blackpool was established, with Tom at the helm. His father Michael kept a guiding eye on it, but also continued managing O'Shea's.

The business is run today by Rachel, Michael's great-great-great-granddaughter, who was delighted to be able to take a stall in the English Market in 2011. One hundred and twenty years later, Healy's Bakery is back in almost the same spot as when it was first established. The stall now sells delicious cakes and pastries, as well as breads and local Cork specialities of seed cake and Chester cake. The business now also specialises in novelty cakes and will make and decorate any cake to any specifications. The most unusual request to date? A 30-tier wedding cake which stood at 22 feet high in 2010 and required 1,440 eggs, 77kg of icing and 32kg of flour.

Healy's Bakery accepts telephone orders on 021-4303466.

Seed Cake

A true Cork favourite, old-fashioned caraway seed cake is also known as 'poor man's Christmas cake'. It was baked traditionally by farmers' wives to celebrate the end of the wheat-sowing season.

Makes 1 loaf

100g/4oz soft butter
100g /4oz caster sugar
2 large eggs
150g/5oz self-raising flour
25g/1oz ground almonds
2–3 tbsp caraway seeds (available from Mr Bell's)
a drop of milk

Preheat your oven to 180°C/355°F/gas mark 4. Grease a 7-inch loaf tin and line the bottom with greaseproof paper. Cream the sugar and the butter together. Beat in the eggs gradually. Mix together the dry ingredients and then fold the dry mixture into the wet mixture. Add a little milk to make it slightly wetter until it drops from a spoon.

Bake in your loaf tin in the middle of the oven for 50–60 minutes. Test it by putting in a skewer – if it comes away clean, the cake is ready.

Tom Healy (left with basket), 1919.

Josephine Healy, 1919.

French Toast with Mascarpone and Berries

A great way of using up old bread and a lovely treat for a leisurely weekend breakfast.

Serves 2

2 free-range eggs
75ml/3fl oz milk
25g/1oz butter
4 slices of day-old bread
icing sugar
mascarpone
berries of your choice

Beat the eggs and milk together in a small bowl and then pour on to a dinner plate – this makes it easier when soaking the bread in the milk/egg mixture. Heat the frying pan and add a knob of butter. Soak the slices of bread – both sides – in the egg and milk mixture. Allow any excess mixture to drip back on to the plate. The bread should be well soaked but not dripping.

Place the bread in the hot pan and turn over as soon as it just browns. Continue like this until all the slices are cooked. Serve with a spoon of mascarpone and some berries. Finish off with a sprinkling of icing sugar.

The Rave Cave

Stalls 9 & 10

Paul Mulvany opened The Rave Cave in the English Market almost thirty years ago. He sells rock and roll memorabilia, baseball caps, Cork t-shirts and rap and hip-hop streetwear. Paul also runs and manages a small art gallery in the Market, which is called, appropriately enough, The Market Gallery. 'It provides an outlet for up-and-coming young Cork artists to exhibit their work,' says Paul, who is a well-known Cork artist himself.

'I eat like a king,' says Paul. 'I buy all the ingredients for my evening meal here in the Market before I go home. Last night I had roast partridge; the night before, calamari; my kids always complain that there is never anything in my fridge, but there doesn't need to be. Each meal I prepare is bought, cooked and consumed on the same day. I try to avoid red meat and I only used my car four times to drive to work last year. I cycled in all the other days. I love working in the Market and meeting people from all over the world. No two days are the same.'

The Meat Centre

Stall 16

Ken Barrett runs the Meat Centre with panache and sells a variety of top-quality meats. He started out with his own stall in the English Market in 1979 and has been ably assisted by the lovely Helen O'Callaghan for the past thirty years. The stall had originally been a flower shop, but Ken obtained permission from the council to change it to a butcher's shop. Whether it is best-quality beef you're after or best-quality advice (on any topic, professional or personal), Ken and Helen can dispense a top-quality portion of both with fun and good humour.

Ken originally hails from a small townland called Ballymagooly, near Mallow, but decided a change was in order after spending his formative years on the family farm, earning the princely sum of 1 shilling per week milking the family herd by hand morning and evening. To this day, Ken swears that the cows had 'moods', and if they were in a bad one they would wait until his bucket was full of milk and then kick it with a hoof, sending all his hard work spilling over the milking parlour floor.

Ken frequently proclaims at the top of his voice that he has 'The best meat in the market!' All of his customers tend to agree. 'The feeding of the animal is all-important,' he says. 'If there is any slight glitch in the feeding of the animal, it will mess up the whole process, and you won't have top-quality meat.'

Ken's Classic Top Rib Roast Beef

Roast beef for Sunday lunch, what could be better? This meal demands that everyone makes time to sit down and enjoy good food and great company. It sets you up for the week ahead.

Serves 4–6

2kg/5lb rib joint of beef
1 tsp mustard
a few grinds of black pepper
5 peeled shallots, or 2 onions, peeled and halved
1 tbsp flour
1 pint of hot stock
salt and pepper

Spread the fatty surface of the beef with a mixture of mustard and black pepper. Place in a roasting dish. Add some peeled shallots or onion halves around the joint to give extra flavour and colour to the gravy.

Preheat the oven to 200°C/390°F/gas mark 4. Place the joint in the hot oven for 15 minutes, then reduce the temperature to 180°C/355°F/gas mark 4 and allow 15 minutes per ½kg/1lb for rare, plus 20 minutes extra for medium or 30 minutes extra for well done. When the meat is cooked, remove from the oven and place on a carving board, cover loosely with tin foil and allow to rest for 30 minutes.

To make the gravy, spoon off the fat from the juices in the roasting dish. (You can use the fat for roasting potatoes – it will keep for up to one week in the fridge or you can freeze it for use at a later date.) Add the flour and stir very quickly over a moderate heat until the juices and the flour have formed a smooth paste.

Add the stock, a little at a time, whisking briskly to ensure everything is well blended. Turn up the heat until the gravy begins to simmer – it will thicken at the same time. If you think the gravy is too thin, let it simmer for a few minutes and it will thicken or reduce. If you think it is too thick, add a little more stock. Taste and season. Serve with the sliced roast.

This beef is delicious with crispy roast potatoes, roast vegetables or a creamy vegetable purée – see perfect roast potatoes recipe on page 257.

Perfect Roast Potatoes

Crisp, golden brown roast potatoes straight from the oven – delicious. Making the perfect roast potatoes isn't difficult, as you can see in this roast potato recipe. If you have a large dinner to prepare and are pushed for time, the potatoes can be half-roasted the day before, then finish off for 20 minutes in a hot oven.

Serves 4

500g/1lb floury potatoes, peeled
4 tbsp goose fat, lard or vegetable oil
salt and pepper

Preheat the oven to 220°C/425°F/gas mark 7. Cut the potatoes into even-sized pieces. Place the potatoes in a saucepan, cover with cold water, add a sprinkle of salt and bring to the boil. Once boiling, lower the heat and simmer for 10 minutes. Drain the potatoes in a colander. Gently shake the colander to fluff the outside of the potatoes.

Heat the fat or oil in a roasting tin until very hot but not burning. Carefully tip the potatoes into the hot fat. Using a tablespoon, coat each potato with the hot fat in the tin; this will help prevent the potatoes from sticking. Return the roasting tin to the hot oven and roast until golden brown and crisp, turning the potatoes from time to time. Cooking time in the oven will take approximately 45 minutes. Serve immediately.

Salad of Spiced Beef with Roasted Pears, Walnuts and Cooleeney Cheese

Christmas and Cork are synonymous with spiced beef. You can't have one without the other! There are two types of spiced beef – a 'wet' spice and a 'dry' spice. Ken Barrett favours a dry spice. 'I have been perfecting a new combination of spices for my beef over the last couple of years,' he says, 'and now at last I finally think I've achieved the most amazing blend. My customers say it's the best spiced beef they've ever tasted – and if my customers are happy, then I'm happy!'

Spiced beef, which is distantly related to its American cousin Pastrami, is a fantastic treat and the aroma of spiced beef throughout the house as it bubbles away in its pot can be summed up in three little words: Christmas is Here! But, there is no good reason to wait for Christmas to come around to indulge in this local Cork delicacy when the Meat Centre supplies spiced beef throughout the year. This recipe is great as a starter or even as a main course at any time of the year.

Serves 4

2kg/4lb Ken Barrett's spiced beef	30ml/1½fl oz sherry vinegar, or white wine vinegar
1 onion	salt and freshly ground black pepper
1 carrot	2 handfuls rocket leaves
1 stick of celery	2 handfuls baby spinach
4 pears	50g/2oz Cooleeney cheese
90ml/3fl oz Irish rapeseed oil	a handful of walnuts, chopped
1 tbsp icing sugar	

The spiced beef needs to be cooked ahead of time, and even better if you can cook it the day before. Put the beef in a large pot of cold water with the onion, carrot and celery stick. Bring to the boil and turn down to a simmer – leave to cook for 2½–3 hours. Allow the meat to cool in the cooking liquor. When the beef has cooled, remove from the pot and slice with a good sharp knife.

To roast the pears, preheat the oven to 180°C/355°F/gas mark 4. Peel, quarter and core the pears. Heat a small roasting pan and add a little olive oil. Place the pears in the roasting tin and cook them in the oven for 4–5 minutes; turn them over after a couple of minutes. Finally, turn the pears right-side-up and sprinkle them with icing sugar and roast again in the oven for about 6–8 minutes, until golden and soft.

To make the salad dressing, whisk the oil into the vinegar and season with salt and cracked pepper.

To serve, combine the salad leaves in a bowl and dress with the salad dressing. Place the leaves on a plate and arrange two slices of the spiced beef on top. Arrange the warm pears around the edges with small slices of the Cooleeney cheese in between. Sprinkle with chopped walnuts to finish.

Best Meats

Stalls 34 & 38

Paul Boyling began trading in the English Market in 1976. Originally from London, Paul had served his apprenticeship with a chain of London butchers during the 1950s. Master butcher John Mansins decided to send Paul to the Smithfield School of Butchery for three days a week over a period of three years in order to perfect his trade. Paul worked in many butchers shops throughout London until he eventually worked his way up to a managerial position. He met and married a Cork woman in 1970 and decided to move to Cork. Paul worked in several Cork butchers before opening his own shop in the English Market in 1976.

He is a master sausage-maker who has accumulated a wealth of traditional sausage recipes over the years and his famous spiced beef has been used by numerous chefs and even featured in one of Gary Rhodes' cookery programmes. Another of Best Meats' specialities is wild rabbit, which is sourced locally in Cork, and celebrity chef Richard Corrigan featured this in one of his cookery programmes.

English Market Wild Rabbit Stew

Rabbit used to be very plentiful in Ireland, but with the outbreak of myxomatosis in the 1950s the rabbit population severely declined and people ceased to eat the meat. Nowadays the countryside is well populated with healthy specimens, making it a viable alternative to red meat. Rabbit is very low in fat and cholesterol and is nutritious and very tasty. Because of this, it is often recommended on special diets for heart patients and people with digestive problems.

Serves 4–6

1 rabbit, cut into portions (ask your butcher to do this for you. (If you have a dog or a cat, they'll go crazy for any leftovers, so ask your butcher for these too and you can cook them separately)

3 tbsp butter

½ cup of well-seasoned flour

1 cup chopped celery

2 medium onions, sliced

2 rashers of bacon

1 bay leaf

2 cups red wine

4 carrots, chopped

4 potatoes, peeled, sliced and diced

½ pint chicken or vegetable stock – use one good stock cube (chicken or vegetable) if you don't have time to make fresh stock

2 tbsp tomato purée

1 tin chopped tomatoes

a couple of sprigs of thyme

salt and pepper

Preheat the oven to 180°C/355°F/gas mark 4. Lightly dredge the rabbit pieces in the seasoned flour, and fry until sealed and slightly browned in a large pan. Take the pieces out and put into a large casserole or ovenproof dish. In the same pan, fry the garlic and onions until just turning brown. Now add the garlic and onions to the casserole dish with the rabbit.

Add the bacon to the pan, fry until crispy and add to the casserole. Pour the stock into the casserole dish and add the wine. Stir all the ingredients together in the casserole dish. Put the covered casserole dish in the oven (if you don't have a lid that fits well then cover the dish snugly with two layers of tin foil). Cook for 20 minutes at 180°C/gas 4 and then reduce the temperature to 150°C/300°F/gas mark 3 and cook for another 1 hour and 20 minutes.

Cook the pasta in a large saucepan of boiling water with a tablespoon of oil added. Pasta cooked with a little oil has a much nicer finished texture than pasta cooked without oil, and it also stops the pasta from sticking together, which can often happen with spaghetti. Stir occasionally, and taste to test after 15–20 minutes. It should be *al dente* (have a little bite to it, not soft and soggy). Strain the pasta into a colander.

When the rabbit casserole is cooked, stir the cooked pasta through it just before serving, and serve sprinkled with shavings of Parmesan cheese. You can easily make 'shavings' by running a vegetable peeler along the length of a portion of Parmesan.

Irish Lamb Stew served with Red Onion and Thyme Scones

Serves 6

1½kg/2½lb mutton shoulder pieces or chump chops
4 medium onions, thickly sliced
6 medium carrots, cut into chunks
4 medium potatoes (floury potatoes are best), cut into chunks
1 medium turnip
3 sticks celery, cut diagonally into large pieces
parsley and thyme, tied together with string
salt and pepper

Put the onions, carrots, turnip and celery into a heavy casserole pot and then place the meat on top. Add the herbs and salt and pepper, cover with cold water and bring to the boil. Skim off any excess fat that may rise to the surface, then lower the heat and place the lid on the pot. Simmer gently for 2 hours and remember the old saying: 'A stew boiled is a stew spoiled'.

For presentation purposes, transfer the stew into an 'oven to table' dish 30 minutes before the end of cooking time, and cover the top of the stew with thinly sliced potatoes brushed with melted butter. Place back in the oven for 30 minutes at 180°C/355°F/gas mark 4.

Ladle the stew into deep bowls and garnish with chopped parsley. Serve with red onion and thyme scones – see the savoury scone recipe on page 266.

Red Onion and Thyme Scones

Makes 10–12 scones

225g/9oz plain flour
4tsp baking powder
½ tsp salt
50g/2oz butter
150ml/5fl oz milk
1 medium egg
1 small red onion, chopped and fried in a little butter
2 tsp chopped thyme

Preheat the oven to 210°C/410°F/gas mark 6 and lightly grease a baking tray. Sift the flour, baking powder and salt into a bowl and rub in the butter, until the mixture resembles breadcrumbs. Stir in the onion and thyme. Finally, add the milk and mix lightly into a soft dough.

Roll the dough out to 1.25cm/½in thickness and cut into rounds. Place on the greased baking tray. Brush the tops with beaten egg and bake for 10–12 minutes or until golden brown.

Cool on a wire rack.

Shepherd's Pie

A firm Irish family favourite. One helping is never enough!

1 medium onion, chopped
2 carrots, chopped
2 tbsp butter
3 tbsp flour
600ml/1 pint of beef stock (or chicken if you prefer)
450g/1lb cooked minced lamb
650g/6–8 large potatoes, mashed
additional butter for the mashed potato
40ml/1fl oz milk
a little grated cheddar cheese (optional)

Peel the potatoes and cut into quarters. Boil the potatoes in boiling salted water for 20 minutes or until cooked. Check with a fork. Strain off the water when they are cooked, season well with salt and pepper, add butter and milk and mash well.

Melt the butter in a saucepan and add the chopped onion. Cover and let sweat for a few minutes, then add the carrots.

Stir in the flour and cook until it is slightly browned, then add the stock and herbs.

Add the cooked meat (which you have fried off in a frying pan) and bring the saucepan to the boil. Reduce the heat and allow to simmer for 10 minutes.

Place the meat mixture in a large pie dish and cover with the mashed potatoes. (You can sprinkle grated cheddar over the top if you wish.) Cook in a medium hot oven 180°C/355°F/gas mark 4 for about 30 minutes.

The Garden

Stalls P1 & P2

The Garden is owned and run by Donal O'Callaghan and Martina Bohrdt. This is their account of how they came to be the custodians of their stall in the English Market.

Early summer of 1998 found us exploring West Cork for a house to raise a family and enough land to grow organic fruit and vegetables for ourselves, with no particular commercial idea in mind. But then we happened on a beautiful-looking place belonging to a French couple. They had already made a name for themselves for their cheeses and, two years before, had also started an organic market-garden on their land, bringing their produce to the English Market at weekends to sell from their stall there. We were smitten, and decided to give it a go.

We didn't expect it to be easy to take over a functioning organic concern with an outlet to be supplied and the expectations of a discriminating customer base to be met, but we were prepared for a steep learning curve and jumped in enthusiastically. Our plan took an unexpected turn though – no sooner had we begun than the Market management announced that the stall would have to open for six days a week instead of its previous two. The work quickly became insurmountable, and it was clear that something had to give in our still new and now sleep-deprived lifestyle. In the three months since starting though, the charm and sense of place of the English Market and its unsurpassed attractiveness as a working environment had crept quietly under our skins and, when we realised that other West Cork organic growers would supply us, we decided to let the farm go and concentrate on the stall.

Since those early beginnings, The Garden has grown with us. It has transformed itself from a small farm outlet to a full-time business, becoming the first certified organic retail outlet in Ireland and receiving the prestigious Bridgestone Award every year since. Despite the many ups and downs of business which we have encountered, it has proved to be a richly rewarding and satisfying experience, augmenting our great interest in good and healthy food. Knowledgeable customers and employees, who have come from every continent, have contributed their cultural tastes and flavours to our own.

Our years in The Garden have taught and shaped us, and we look forward to the changes and adaptations that the future will require. Life is good in The Garden!

271

Carrot Soup

A healthy and flavoursome soup with an unusual hint of mandarin. Great served for lunch or as an easy and nutritious supper.

Serves 4–6

1 bulb garlic, chopped

1 large pepper, any colour, chopped

700g carrots, cleaned and chopped

300g celeriac, chopped

1 tsp ground coriander

½ tsp ground cumin

½ tsp turmeric powder

1.8 litres/3½ pints meat or vegetable stock

handful of leaf coriander

1 mandarin, juiced

salt

lemon juice

In a saucepan heat the oil and add the garlic and pepper. Cook over a medium heat for 8–10 minutes. Then add the carrots, celeriac, coriander, cumin and turmeric and cook for 5 minutes, stirring frequently (add more oil if necessary to prevent burning).

Add the meat or vegetable stock. Cover the pot and simmer until the vegetables are tender. Add a good handful of leaf coriander and the juice of 1 mandarin and purée in a blender. Add salt and lemon juice to taste.

Multi-veg Coleslaw

Packed full of healthy goodness, a great side dish with a difference. You'll get more than your 'five-a-day' from this delicious recipe alone.

Serves 6

½ large bulb of fennel
4 medium carrots
½ small head cauliflower
⅓–½ head of white cabbage
150g/5oz French beans
½ pepper (any colour)
400g pistachios, chopped
1–2 handfuls of dried cranberries
mayonnaise to mix
salt

In a food processor coarsely grate the fennel, carrots, cauliflower and cabbage. Cook the French beans, drain well and cut into bite-sized pieces. Dice the pepper into small pieces. Combine all the ingredients and place them in a colander for 20 minutes to drain off most of the juices (which can be reserved for smoothies and other recipes).

Place the vegetables in a bowl, add the pistachios and the dried cranberries and mix in as much good-quality mayonnaise as required. Add salt to taste and serve.

This recipe can also be made with a lemon, honey, mustard and olive oil salad dressing if you don't like mayonnaise.

Pots and Pans

Stall 4a

T his is a compact stall selling cooking utensils, saucepans, cookware, cutlery, glassware and cleaning implements. Everything you could possibly need for the kitchen and all at the keenest of prices can be found at Pots and Pans.

The Benefits of Hanging Meat

In general, meat is tenderised by allowing it to 'hang' for a period of time. Recently the term 'hanging' has been replaced by the term 'dry-ageing', probably because it sounds more politically correct, but the butchers in the English Market still refer to the process as 'hanging'.

Hanging or dry-ageing (whichever you prefer) is the process which allows the connective tissue to be broken down by natural enzymes, which in turn results in the meat becoming more tender. Another effect which hanging has on the meat is that of allowing excess water to evaporate away, which concentrates and improves the overall flavour of the meat. It takes at least eleven days before you see much improvement in the flavour of the meat through the process of hanging and some of the best meat is hung for at least twenty-one days. Many of the butchers in the English Market will hang their meat for a minimum of twenty-four days, but in general the majority will hang their meat for some time between twenty-four to thirty days.

A traditional butcher always takes more care and interest in hanging meat. After all, meat is his speciality. Supermarkets, however, are very often not prepared to take up valuable cold storage space so that the product can improve when they can just as easily sell it on quickly and make their profit. Also, as up to 20 per cent of the weight of the meat may be lost in the hanging process as much of the moisture in the meat evaporates away, this is another major factor which contributes to large supermarket chains not being prepared to invest in the process. This loss of excess moisture results in meat of superior tenderness and flavour but, as meat is sold by weight, this means a smaller profit margin for the supermarket chain.

It is essential that the cut of meat that is hung has to merit the time invested in it, so the meat must have an adequate covering of outside fat or it will deteriorate quickly, especially if held for more than five days. Consequently, lamb and veal are usually hung for a maximum of five days, or even less, as they do not have an adequate covering of fat, but this meat comes from young animals, so it is likely to be more tender. Beef and mutton, however, benefit from a lengthier hanging period. Also, a good cut of meat should contain a certain amount of fat running through it – this is known as marbling. If the meat is not well marbled, it may not be worth hanging for an extended period.

Temperature is all-important for the process of hanging to be successful. Too warm and the meat will spoil, too cold and the meat may freeze, which halts the entire process and so defeats the purpose.

Well-hung meat will be dark in colour and may even be slightly purplish. Many people mistake this as a bad sign and prefer to opt for meat which is bright red in colour. However, the brighter and redder the meat is, the less time it has been hanging, and so it will not be as tender or flavoursome as another piece of meat on the same counter which may be dark red with a purplish hue. A wise meat shopper will always opt for the latter.

If you are curious or would like to find out more about hanging meat, just ask any butcher in the English Market and they will be happy to explain and demonstrate if they are not too busy.

Fruit Boost

Stall 14

Eddie Vaughan opened his stall called Fruit Boost in the English Market in June 2004. It was the first juice bar to open in Cork. 'We had first seen the concept in the US,' says Eddie, 'and having looked at many locations, I came to the conclusion that the English Market would be an ideal location for Cork's first juice bar. It's in the heart of the city centre, has a strong tradition of fresh unadulterated food and is popular with locals and tourists alike.'

Fruit Boost sells a range of juices and smoothies, from the slightly unusual Ginger Spice (carrot, apple and ginger) to the ever-popular Strawberry Heaven (apple, banana, strawberry and yoghurt). Fruit Boost juices and smoothies are always juiced at the time of order to give optimum freshness. 'The vitamins and minerals in juices get oxidised over time, so it's important to make fresh at the time of order,' Eddie explains.

Unlike other juice bars, Fruit Boost never uses concentrates, so the fresh fruit you see at the stall is the same fruit that will be in your juice or smoothie five minutes later. 'The yoghurt we use is sourced locally and is both low-fat and pro-biotic,' says Eddie. 'We make a big effort to source locally whenever possible. Our flapjacks are from Stable Diet in Wexford and we only use Irish-grown strawberries in our fruit salads.'

Tropical Storm Smoothie

Eddie's recipe below will make 1 litre of Tropical Storm, a popular smoothie at the Fruit Boost stall, especially in the summer months. For juices and smoothies, you generally need two pieces of equipment – a juicer and a blender.

Serves 4

juice of 4 oranges
1 banana
¼ fresh pineapple
⅓ fresh mango, peeled
6 strawberries
½l/18fl oz frozen natural yoghurt

Squeeze 4 oranges, giving approximately 320ml/½ pint juice.

Add 1 whole banana to the blender. Remove the skin from a pineapple, then cut it into circular sections and from there into smaller pieces. Add a quarter of the pineapple to the blender. Remove the mango skin with a potato peeler, taking care as mangos can be slippery. Add one-third of the mango to the blender. Next, add six strawberries to the blender. Finally, add the yoghurt. If you don't have frozen yoghurt, you can freeze a tub in your home freezer and use this. The cold temperature of the frozen yoghurt makes the smoothie nice and thick and helps bring out the flavour of the individual fruits. Blend until smooth.

Serve in 4 glasses.

Fresh Fruit Salad

A delicious and healthy alternative to cake or pudding: sweet, juicy and refreshingly good.

Serves 4

2 tbsp of blueberries
¼ pineapple, peeled and diced
1 mango, peeled and diced
1 banana, sliced
2 kiwi, peeled and sliced
½ star fruit, sliced
8 strawberries, quartered
125ml/4fl oz crème fraîche
1 tsp honey
4 sprigs fresh mint

For the syrup
350ml/½ pint orange juice
1 tbsp sugar

Make the syrup first by placing the orange juice and sugar in a pot and bringing to the boil. Simmer for about 5 minutes. Take off the heat and leave to cool for about 30 minutes. Place all the fruits in a bowl and, when the syrup has cooled, pour it over the fruits. Next mix the crème fraîche and honey together in a bowl.

To serve place 2 tablespoons of the crème fraîche and honey in a small bowl and add the sprigs of mint on top for a garnish. Place in the centre of a large serving bowl and surround with fruit salad.

This recipe is tastier if the fruit salad is prepared at least 2 hours before serving and placed in the fridge as this allows all the flavours to infuse.

William Martin

Stall 41

William Martin has seen a lot of changes in the English Market since he began working at Sheehan's fish stall over forty-three years ago. Back then, there were at least sixteen fish stalls in the market, today only three remain, one of which belongs to William. After Sheehan's, William got a position at Finbarr Horgan's fish stall, where he perfected his trade as a fishmonger. William says he works harder today than in days gone by, as the market always closed at midday on Mondays and Wednesdays. Today he works Monday to Saturday and business comes at a steady rate, but thirty years ago almost all the fish-buying was done on Thursday or Friday mornings, as all Catholics were expected to abstain from meat on Fridays and chicken was too expensive to be seen as an alternative then. For William, business has always been better in times of financial recession, as people are on the lookout for a bargain, and William guarantees that he will not be beaten on price.

William's Seafood Chowder

What could be more welcoming on a cold winter's day than a delicious bowl of freshly-made chowder? William recommends that you serve this unforgettable chowder with a large slice of brown bread.

50g/2oz butter
1 large onion, sliced
4 rashers of smoked bacon, chopped up small
250ml/9fl oz whole milk
200ml/7fl oz single cream
300ml/½ pint fish stock
1 large potato, peeled and cut into cubes
450g/1lb William's seafood mix
100g/3–4 oz spinach, shredded
salt and freshly ground black pepper
2 tbsp chopped parsley to garnish
crusty bread, to serve

Melt the butter in a frying pan over a low heat. Add the onion and fry for 8–10 minutes, until very soft but not coloured. Add the bacon and cook for 5 more minutes.

Add the milk, cream, stock and potatoes. Bring to the boil, then reduce to a simmer for 10 minutes. Add William's seafood mix and cover the pan. Simmer for 8–10 minutes, until the fish is completely cooked through.

Add the spinach and season to taste with salt and freshly ground black pepper.
Pour into bowls, sprinkle a little chopped parsley on top and serve with crusty bread.

William's Fish Cakes

These fish cakes are very simple to make and taste great. They work very well as a delicious starter or, if you make them 'bite-sized', they can be served as canapés.

3 large potatoes
1 red onion
200g/7oz fresh fish fillets
1tsp wholegrain mustard
1 bunch of parsley
2 eggs
200g/7oz flour
salt and pepper
200g fresh breadcrumbs
100ml/3fl oz milk
oil for frying
lemon wedges

Peel and wash the potatoes and cut into even-sized pieces. Boil them in a saucepan of boiling water with a good pinch of salt. When the potatoes have cooked (20 minutes or so, check with a fork), strain them and mash with milk and butter until smooth. Set aside and allow to cool.

Peel and dice the red onion finely. Cut the fish into pieces, about the size of your thumb. Now, mix the fish, mashed potatoes, red onion, wholegrain mustard, chopped parsley, salt and pepper. Form the mixture into individual fish cakes about the size of the palm of your hand – coat your hands with flour before moulding each fish cake, otherwise things become hopelessly sticky! Beat the eggs in a bowl until smooth. Using two plates, place 3 tablespoons of flour on one, then the fresh breadcrumbs on the other. Now, dip each cake first into the flour, then into the beaten eggs and finally into the breadcrumbs, making sure to coat both sides evenly.

Heat a splash of olive oil in a frying pan and fry the fish cakes on each side for two minutes, or until golden. Place the fish cakes in an ovenproof dish and put in the oven for ten minutes at 180°C/355°F/ gas mark 4. Serve with a wedge of lemon.

Pat O'Connell:
My English Market

Pat O'Connell is the owner stallholder of Kay O'Connell's
Fish Stall in The English Market.

One of my earliest childhood memories is of helping my mother Kathleen to
push a trolley of fish along the Grand Parade en route to our stall in the English
Market. That would have been around 1962, and at that time fish auctions were
held every morning at Clayton Love's on the Coal Quay. The fish would be
bought at the auction and then wheeled over on trolleys to the Market. For a
five-year-old, the English Market was both an adventurous playground and a
terrifying ordeal all at the same time, what with hefty sides of beef being carried
on the shoulders of butchers to be weighed at the communal scales next to
Bertie Bagnall's fruit and veg stall, trolleys full of beady-eyed fish being wheeled
to the fish stalls, tripe and drisheen being brought in in barrels and pigs' heads
smiling out at you from fresh meat counters.

In some ways today's English Market is very different from the Market of my
childhood and yet in many, many ways it hasn't changed at all. Today's Market
has a much wider variety of produce; there is still an incredible array of fish,
meat and veg but these are now sold alongside cheeses, olives, spices, chocolates
and almost any food you can think of. The Market now also has a fabulous
restaurant upstairs, as well as supplying most of the best restaurants in the city.
Cork's English Market has been on the go for over 200 years and it has survived
recession, depression, fires and boom times.

The level of hygiene, presentation and service today is far superior to what was
accepted as the norm in 1962 and today the English Market consistently ranks
as one of the top markets in Europe. To me, a good market reflects the character
and culture of its city. Cork city is known as the Rebel City, a description that
conjures up images of a fiery character, passion and a willingness to 'buck the

trend'. The English Market traders have all of these traits in abundance, which gives the Market its unique character, atmosphere and sense of fun. But don't be fooled. These traders take their business and their products very seriously and are extremely passionate about what they do; it's what has ensured the survival of the Market for over 200 years. *Dá mhéid a athraíonn rudaí sea is mó a fhanann siad mar a bhí* – the more things change, the more they remain the same.

Index

vinegar (white wine)
    Bone Marrow with Boxty 237

W

walnuts
    Apple Cake 63
    Salad of Spiced Beef with Roasted Pears, Walnuts and
        Cooleeney Cheese 258
whiskey
    Irish Coffee 74
    Seared Ballycotton Scallops with Rashers of Bacon in
        an Irish Whiskey Cream Sauce 161
white pudding
    White Pudding and Orchard Apple Tartlets 6
wine
    Ashley O'Neill's Rib-Eye Steak on a Red Wine
        Reduction with Balsamic Onions, Wild
        Mushrooms and Hand-Cut Potato Chips 202

English Market Wild Rabbit Stew 262
Fillets of Ostrich with Port and Cranberry Sauce 191
O'Connell's Lemon Sole Fillets with Dublin Bay
    Prawns 96
Red Wine Jus 68
Roast Goose with Apples and Prune Compote 146
Spring Rosé Pork Steak 71
Supreme Chicken Surprise 69
wine vinegar
    Bone Marrow with Boxty 237
    Salad of Spiced Beef with Roasted Pears, Walnuts and
        Cooleeney Cheese 258

Y

yoghurt
    Easy Mango and Passion Fruit Mousse 85
    Kangaroo Fillet with Sweet Parsnips 192
    Tropical Storm Smoothie 282

Bibliography

Allen, Darina, *Irish Traditional Cooking* (Gill & Macmillan, Dublin 1995)

Anderson, Glynn, and John McGlaughlin, *Farmhouse Cheeses of Ireland: A Celebration* (The Collins Press, 2011)

Bord Bia, *Your Guide to Irish Farmhouse Cheeses* (Bord Bia, Dublin 2011)

Ó Drisceoil, Diarmuid, and Donal Ó Drisceoil, *Serving a City: The Story of Cork's English Market* (The Collins Press, 2005)

O'Loan, J., *A History of Early Irish Farming* (Department of Agriculture and Fisheries, 1965)

Mrs Beeton's Book of Household Management (1861)

Solinus, Gaius Julius, *Collectanea Rerum Memorabilianum* (University of Texas Press, Austin, Texas, 2000)

Useful Websites

www.recipesfromtheenglishmarket.com

Bord Bia, the Irish food board	www.bordbia.ie
CÁIS (Ireland)	www.irishcheese.ie
Good Food Ireland	www.goodfoodireland.ie
Organic Grower's Association of Ireland	www.irishorganic.ie
Irish seafood	www.iasc.ie

Acknowledgements

Firstly, a huge 'thank you' to all the traders in the English Market who took part in the making of this book – without you there would be no book. Thank you for all your encouragement, support and warmth. I am a very fortunate woman to have made such firm friends. Many thanks also to Cork City Council.

Thank you to my girls, Jennifer, Hazel, Grace and Jeanann.

Thank you Louis Eden, Jedrzej Niezgoda and Jason Town for your very wonderful and talented photography.

Thank you to Mike Collins and Maria O'Donovan of Cork University Press for saying: 'Let's do it'!

Thank you to Bord Bia for your assistance.

Thank you to Captain Barry O'Driscoll for some spectacularly great recipes, *cáint agus craic*. Thank you also to Laura and Barry Jr. – love always.

For 'Best Supporting Actress in a Real Life Drama' the Oscar goes to . . . Carina Wilson O'Halloran!... Thank you, Carina!

Thank you to Paul and Val Griffin for letting me raid your Aladdin's cave of family heirlooms.

Thank you to my parents, Michael and Natalie. And apologies for my whirlwind visits which ended with me leaving with china, kitchen utensils or silverwear tucked under my arm to facilitate various photo shoots. Also, sorry for taking your favourite knife, Dad.

Thank you Natalie and Nick for all your support, encouragement and artistic involvement. www.westcorkartist.com.

Míle buíchous to Veronica Steele, Pat O'Connell, Mairéad Lavery, Nigel O'Mahony and Rory Conner for your fantastic contributions. I hope that we can all get around a table and enjoy an English Market Feast together – what a night that would be!

Míle buíchous to Aonghus Ó hAmhain for the *cúpla focal*.

Lastly, a very big Thank You to the ladies (and young man) from Carrigaline Parish who rose to the challenge of an epic morning of cake-baking and an afternoon of cake photography. How wonderful it is to discover that you're never too old to make new friends! Thank you, Finola Stephens and Diarmuid Hurley, Niamh Dennehy, Tricia O'Donovan, Margaret Mullarkey, Grace Gallagher and Siobhan Kelly – ace cake-bakers, great storytellers (and epic tea-drinkers) one and all!

Thank you to John Brennan. Even though I only met you once, John (on the outset of my journey), you were with me all the way – a true Virgil.

Notes

Notes

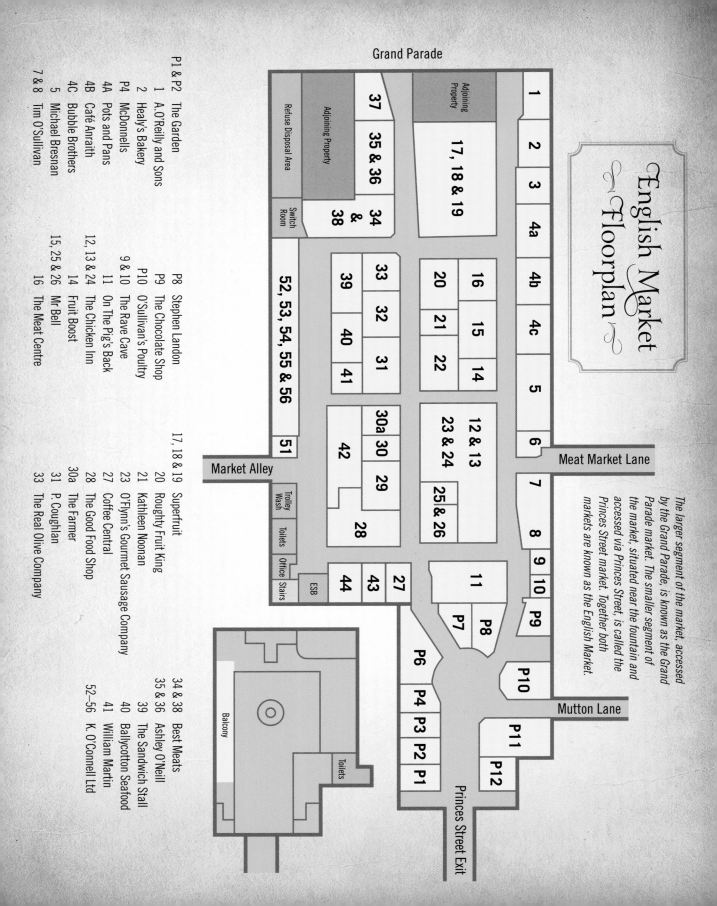

English Market Floorplan

Grand Parade

The larger segment of the market, accessed by the Grand Parade, is known as the Grand Parade market. The smaller segment of the market, situated near the fountain and accessed via Princes Street, is called the Princes Street market. Together both markets are known as the English Market.

Meat Market Lane

Mutton Lane

Princes Street Exit

Market Alley

Refuse Disposal Area

Adjoining Property

Adjoining Property

Switch Room

Balcony

Toilets

Trolley Wash

Toilets

Office

Stairs

ESB

Stall listings

P1 & P2 — The Garden
1 — A.O'Reilly and Sons
2 — Healy's Bakery
P4 — McDonnells
4A — Pots and Pans
4B — Café Anraith
4C — Bubble Brothers
5 — Michael Bresnan
7 & 8 — Tim O'Sullivan

P8 — Stephen Landon
P9 — The Chocolate Shop
P10 — O'Sullivan's Poultry
9 & 10 — The Rave Cave
11 — On The Pig's Back
12, 13 & 24 — The Chicken Inn
14 — Fruit Boost
15, 25 & 26 — Mr Bell
16 — The Meat Centre

17, 18 & 19 — Superfruit
20 — Roughty Fruit King
21 — Kathleen Noonan
23 — O'Flynn's Gourmet Sausage Company
27 — Coffee Central
28 — The Good Food Shop
30a — The Farmer
31 — P. Coughlan
33 — The Real Olive Company

34 & 38 — Best Meats
35 & 36 — Ashley O'Neill
39 — The Sandwich Stall
40 — Ballycotton Seafood
41 — William Martin
52–56 — K. O'Connell Ltd